KARPATHOS

Thodoris Kiousis

CONTENTS

- **5** Introduction
- **7** Geography
- **11** Geology
- **13** Flora & Fauna
- **15** Getting There
- **17** Getting Around
- **21** History
- **33** Folklore – Culture
- **43** Economy
- **45** Settlements

Sight	**69**
Routes of the island	**89**
Alternative Tourism	**115**
Beaches	**127**
Local Cuisine - Shopping	**147**
Accommodation	**151**
Useful Telephone Numbers	**157**
Afterword	**158**
Bibliography	**160**

CONTRIBUTORS

PUBLISHER
Apostolis Nakas

RESEARCH – TEXT
Thodoris Kiousis

PHOTOGRAPHIC MATERIAL
Thodoris Kiousis

EDITOR
Sofia Politou-Ververi

DESIGN – LAYOUT
Pelagia Baka

GIS MAPPING
George Benekos

I would very much appreciate it if you sent me your remarks, suggestions and comments on the present travel guide at: **tedkappa@hotmail.com**
Thank you all, Thodorís Kioúsis

© **NAKAS ROAD CARTOGRAPHY**　　　　　　　　　　**2nd Edition, 2018**

The present publication is copyright of NAKAS GROUP. Any form of scanning, copying, photographing or reproducing the entire or part of this publication without the written permission of NAKAS GROUP is strictly forbidden. Any breach of copyright will be prosecuted by NAKAS GROUP, according to the copyright law. In order to safeguard and consolidate their rights, the publisher has herein included certain intentional errors so that any form of reproduction can be easily recognized.

Member of

23th km of Marathonos Avenue, Rafina, Attica, Greece 19009, Tel.: +30 22940 79816
info@road.gr • **www.road.gr**

INTRODUCTION

Kárpathos is one of the remotest parts and one of the most beautiful islands of Greece! It is very rare for a small Aegean island to include so many contrasts and combinations, not only in the nature but also in the cultural traditions of the locals. The oblong size and the position of the island between the Dodecanese and Crete make it look like a bridge. The natural beauty of the entire island is unique from the barren tops of the north part to the green slopes of Mt. Lástos at the centre of the island and from that point to the fertile plain of Afiártis to the south. From Saría, the little island of the pirates to the north, as far as the wild Diakóftis to the south, which serves as the guard of the Libyan Sea, the island is full of magical beaches with emerald waters. However, the most fascinating sight of all is the villages and the people of Kárpathos. The capital, the cosmopolitan Pigádia with the big and modern hotels and the pretty little taverns, is full of scenic alleys for lovely evening walks by the sea. Visit the historic Menetés with the hospitable inhabitants, Arkása with its monuments, and the four inland villages of Apéri, Voláda, Óthos and Pylés, and do not fail to see Mesochóri, which overlooks the open sea to the west, and Spóa with its proud people to the east, and, finally, the famous village of Olympos to the north, a living cultural museum where the visitor meets women wearing traditional costumes and thinks that time has stopped in the past...

There are remarkable tourist infrastructures meeting all modern requirements of the visitors. There are big and up-to-date hotels as well as smaller accommodation facilities mainly in the capital but also in the other settlements. Very good markets with local products, souvenirs, brands and more advanced choices. KTEL public buses and a big number of taxis, together with rented cars, will help you travel along the extensive and charming road network of the island. The local cuisine is a souvenir on its own. Historical monuments and several (!) museums exist on the island! Alternative tourism is rapidly developing: here you can find one of the best preserved hiking networks running along the welcoming mountains and the south coasts, which serve as reference points for surfers. There are also fascinating paths for mountain biking and opportunities for climbing and diving... You can find anything you want on this little island and it is very difficult for even the most demanding visitor to leave the island unsatisfied! So, let's go and meet Kárpathos!

In order to better understand the information included in this guide, you should be provided with the respective new map (No. 201) Kárpathos – Kásos by Nakas ROAD Cartography.

THODORIS KIOUSIS

ACKNOWLEDGMENTS

Publishers Giorgos and Apostolis Nakas

Father Dimitrios Zagoras,
priest at the cathedral of Kárpathos and Kásos

Father Ioannis Diakogeorgiou,
priest at the Church of Koímisi tis Theotókou of Olympos

Dinos Protopappas, Deputy Mayor of Kárpathos

Manolis Kritsiotis, owner of ANEMOS – ION CLUB

Captain Giorgos Protopappas from Diafáni

Nikos Vasilas of the Club of Mountain
and Sea Friends of Kárpathos

Local officers of the Hellenic Coast Guard

Venetia Pitta (Ms) of the museum of Arkása

Kalliroe Georgiou (Ms), publisher of Karpathiakí newspaper

Popi Hatzidaki (Ms) from Menetés

Ellada (Ms) and Giorgos Lyristis from Arkása

Anna Annousi (Ms) from Voláda

My cousins, Paris and Athena Skamangas, from Voláda

My good friend Nikos Alexiou from Pigádia

GEOGRAPHY

The border island of Kárpathos is situated on the SE corner of the Greek territory, between Crete and Rhodes, and is watered by the Karpathian Sea. It is the second largest island of the cluster of the Dodecanese. The island of Kásos is within only 3 miles to the SW. The notional framework surrounding Kárpathos is specified by the coordinates E27°3' to E27°14' and W35°54' to W35°23'. The island covers an area of 302.15 square kilometres and its coastlines are 160 km long. You can imagine it like a sword

GEOGRAPHY

A journey in the Aegean sea

or an upturned exclamation mark! The narrowest point is in the area of the village of Spóa and the maximum width between the two coasts is 6 km. The longest distance from the north **canal of Saría** to the south **Cape Kastello** is 48 km. The island -with the exception of the south part- is covered by mountains, with the highest point being **Kalí Límni (1,215 m)** of **Mount Lástos**, which dominates the centre of the island. The mountains of Kefálas (537 m) and Hómalis (686 m) rise to the south, while north Kárpathos accommodates the peaks of **Profítis Ilías (719 m)** and Orkýlli (713 m). There are flat areas to the south, near **Afiártis**, and two plateaus in **Mount Lástos**, Sitaraína to the south and Avlóna to the north. Kárpathos has no rivers but only dozens of torrents and little streams, mainly to the south. There are several islets and skerries around the island, which belong to Kárpathos: Míra, Prassonísi, Nísaros, Diakóftis, Halkiás, Sókastro, Astakída, Astakidópoulo, Ammoúdi and, of course, the islet of **Saría**.

The climate is temperate Mediterranean. In the summer, the etesian winds that blow in the Aegean reduce high temperatures to moderate levels. The average summer temperature is 29°C. Humidity is somewhat increased due to the sea, while rainfall in winter is rather limited.

Together with Kásos, the island forms the province of Kárpathos of the Prefecture of the Dodecanese (South Aegean Region) and includes one municipality with two municipal units. According to the 2011 census, the population is 7,111 people. The capital of the island is Pigádia and the municipal unit of the capital also includes the villages of **Apéri, Voláda, Óthos, Pylés, Arkása, Menetés, Mesochóri, Spóa** as well as the little settlements of **Lefkós, Foiníki, Lákkos Ammoopís** and **Kípos Afiárti**. The second municipal unit is **Olympos**, to the north of the island, which also includes its port, **Diafáni**, and **Avlóna**, the small rural settlement of its breadbasket.

A journey in the Aegean sea

GEOLOGY

Kárpathos belongs to the geotectonic zones of External Hellenides, although it is also related to the Tauride tectonic belt of SW Asia Minor. It shares a common geological history with the other Aegean Islands. They are the products of successive subsidence and emersion of Aegeis, the land that covered the area of the current archipelago millions of years ago. In the north part of the island as well as in the little islet of Saría there is an indigenous carbonic unit of the Cretaceous and the Eocene periods, which is also repeated in the area of the mountains of Agkynára and Profítis Ilías on the east coasts, between Vróntis and Kyrá Panagiá. The part from Olympos to Spóa and Mesochóri as well as the central part of the island with all the villages includes Eocene flysch. The mountain bulk of Lástos consists of limestone of the Triassic period. Finally, quaternary rocks can be found in the south part.

Mainly due to the flysch of its subsoil, Kárpathos has dozens of springs with top quality fresh water as well as plenty of water bores. There are so many water springs that every village has its own, as it happens in Mertónas (the main source of water for Pigádia), Katódio, Fléa of Arkása, Mastrominás of Mesochóri, Agios Nikólaos of Voláda, Lái of Menetés and in several other places.

EARTHQUAKES AND TSUNAMIS IN KARPATHOS

According to mythology, Kárpathos was the place where the Titan Iapetós, the brother of Encélados (meaning earthquake), lived. This proves that such dreadful natural phenomena must have occurred in the geological history of the island. Around midday of February 9, 1948, after the mighty earthquake of 7.1R that shook the island to its core, a tsunami 20 m tall overwhelmed mainly the port of Pigádia. Reports say that the water rushed away three times before it finally returned and proceeded by 150 metres into the shore. Luckily enough, there were only material damages and no casualties. On January 22, 2002, an earthquake 6.3R, whose focus was 90 km under the sea to the NW of Kárpathos, terrified the locals but neither damages nor casualties were reported.

GEOLOGY

Limniótis Cave *(photo: Club of Mountain and Sea Friends of Kárpathos)*

Kárpathos has a large number of remarkable caves with amazing stalagmites and stalactites. The most impressive of them is the cave of Limniótis, along the road to the beach of Aháta. Another beautiful cave can be found in the area of Vroukoúnta, which accommodates the church of Agios Ioánnis, as well as at Mýloi, near the village of Pigádia, where you can admire the cave of Poseidon. Unfortunately, none of them has been developed.

Water facilities at Mertónas springs

A journey in the Aegean sea

FLORA AND FAUNA

Kárpathos is a natural botanical garden thanks to at least 900 species of rare flora, many of which are native to the island. In particular: 922 species of plants have been recorded, with 66 of them being native to Greece, 28 native to the phytogeographical region of Crete - Kásos - Kárpathos - Saría, in which Kárpathos is incorporated with regard to its flora, while another 9 species are exclusively native to Kárpathos *(Ricotia isatoides, Trifolium barbeyi, Dianthus fruticosus ssp. carpathus, Silene ammophila ssp. carpathae, Silene insularis, Carthamus rechingeri, Origanum vetteri, Limonium carpathum, Ophrys aegaea aegaea)*. The most typical plant-tree of Kárpathos is the pine species pinus brutia, which covers the slopes of the central and north island. There is also extensive scrub vegetation, with most common representatives being the usual shrubs of the Aegean, such as rockrose, thorny burnet, genista, lavender, thyme, oregano and milkweed. The maquis of Kárpathos includes kermes oak, mock privet, lentisk, wild olive, autumn heather, bear-

Picture of Karpathos Diving Center

berry, Judas tree and myrtle. It should be underlined that both the central part of the island around Mt. Lástos and the north part, from the village of Olympos to the island of Saría, are areas protected by the Natura environmental network.

The maritime fauna of the island is mainly described by the famous Mediterranean monk seal monachus monachus, which lives mainly in the sea caves of the north part of Kárpathos and on the island of Saría. A special mention should be made of the renowned parrotfish of Kárpathos, which has been known since antiquity! Audouin's gulls, yellow-legged gulls and shags search for food in local waters. There is also a rich variety of wild birds, including Eleonora's falcons, Cory's shearwaters, long-legged buzzards, kestrels, Sardinian warblers and chukar partridges as well as more common and smaller species like blue rock thrushes, stonechats and goldfinches. Hares, martens and several other rodents are included in local fauna. The island is home to 75 species of snails and two native amphibians, the frog and the salamander of Kárpathos, which live only in the north part of the island. The most common reptiles are the non-venomous Caspian whipsnake with a length of up to 2 metres, and the lizards Mediterranean house gecko, European copper skink and Kotschy's gecko. Last but not least, the Aegean cat, whose presence is very common in Kárpathos as in most islands of the Greek archipelago!

THE KARPATHIAN HAREHOUND!

Gun dogs of high reputation and ability to hunt mainly hares used to live as native species in Kárpathos until a few decades ago. The first blow to the friendly animals was the fact that they were counted and then the heavy taxes imposed on their owners by the Italian administration in 1923. They finally disappeared in 1954 following an order for their elimination by the Hellenic Gendarmerie. The reason remains unknown although it must be attributed to the game licence issued the same year by the Greek authorities to 300 Italian hunters-visitors. You see, the Karpathian bloodhound was a serious competitor… That wonderful dog had a sharp muzzle, medium height, narrow waist, short hair, usually white colour with a black nose and, the most important of all, a lovable character!

GETTING THERE

By boat

Kárpathos has two ports: the main port at the capital of Pigádia, which serves sea connections to Diafáni of Kárpathos (16 miles), Hálki (50 miles), Rhodes (82 miles), Kos (152 miles) and Kásos (21 miles), Siteía of Crete (66 miles), Iráklio of Crete (118 miles), Anáfi (102 miles, Santoríni (130 miles), Mílos (190 miles) and Piraeus (260 miles). The second port of the island is Diafáni, the port of Olympos to the north of the island, which serves almost the same sea connections with the exception of the route Piraeus – Santoríni – Kos – Rhodes – Pigádia.

There is a third port to the west of the island called Foiníki, which serves as the port of Arkása. Finally, Agios Nikólaos is the small picturesque port of Spóa.

The sea connections of Kárpathos are one of the most serious problems for the locals. The long voyage to Piraeus, lasting an average of 20 hours, and the great age of the ships explain the problem. Furthermore, the lack of regular local connections with Rhodes and the other Dodecanese islands deteriorates the problems the locals have with communications. The sea connections between Kárpathos and Piraeus and the other islands at the moment the present guide was being written (winter 2016 - 2017) were as follows:

1) Piraeus - Mílos - Santoríni - Anáfi - Irákleio of Crete - Siteía of Crete - Kásos - **Pigádia of Kárpathos - Diafáni of Kárpathos** - Hálki - Rhodes (once a week, 24h 30').

2) Piraeus - Santoríni - Anáfi - Kásos - **Pigádia of Kárpathos - Diafáni of Kárpathos** - Hálki - Rhodes (once a week, 19h).

3a) Piraeus - Samos - Kos - Rhodes - **Pigádia of Kárpathos** (once a week, 20h).

or **3b)** Piraeus - Pátmos - Leipsoí - Léros - Kálymnos - Kos - Sými - Rhodes - **Pigádia of Kárpathos** (once a week, 20h 30').

4) Kásos - **Pigádia of Kárpathos** (daily, 1h 15'. The ship carries only passengers).

The main port of Karpathos at Pigádia

KARPATHOS

By plane

The airport (IATA code: AOK) is in the southernmost part of the island, in the area of Afiártis, within 16 km from the capital of Pigádia. It is an ultramodern facility with auxiliary spaces of 12,500 square metres, parking areas and one of the longest runways in the Balkans (2,400 m)! It was inaugurated in 1970 and was fully renovated in 2009. There are several daily flights (in the summer there are more) mainly served by Olympic Air / Aegean, but also by Sky Express and Astra Airlines, which connect Kárpathos with Athens (duration 1h 5'), Rhodes, Kásos (one of the quickest fights in the world, lasting 5 minutes), Siteía of Crete, and Thessaloniki. Apart from the regular connections within Greece, the airport of Kárpathos also serves lots of flights from abroad (Denmark, Sweden, Norway, the Netherlands, Italy, Poland, Austria, the Czech Republic, Slovakia, Slovenia, Serbia, Israel, Cyprus).

Do not forget that the airport of Kárpathos includes military facilities and, as a result, photographs are prohibited in the area!

The airport building at Afiártis

By boat

Next to the main port of Pigádia (N35°30'52 E27°12'35) there is a new marina for cruisers, accommodating approximately 50 vessels and offering water, electricity and toilets. Fuel is supplied by road tankers from a nearby petrol station (Tel.: 2245023114). The marina is perfectly protected from the wind and port dues are very reasonable. Communication with Port Authorities is in VHF channel 12 (channel 16 only for emergencies). Channels 23 of Astypálaia, 01 of Rhodes and 85 of Siteía provide the weather report for the Karpathian Sea through Olympia Radio.

Apart from Pigádia, you can also find jetties at the port of
Diafáni (N35°45'23, E27°12'44),
Foiníki (N35°29'28, E27°07'01),
Lefkós (N35°35'08, E27°04'12),
and in the cove of Trístomo (N35°49'15, E27°12'16).

Marina for cruisers at Pigádia

GETTING AROUND

Public Bus

Public transport is provided by the local KTEL service of Kárpathos with its several buses that serve almost the entire road network of the island. The service is based along the main road of Pigádia and bus fares are very reasonable. In the summer, communication is very frequent. Because bus routes and destinations often change and increase in number, here are the 9 main routes that operated in the summer of 2016 from the starting point of Pigádia:

1) Olympos, Diafáni
2) Menetés, Arkása, Foiníki, Lefkós
3) Kyrá Panagiá, Ápella
4) Spóa, Mesochóri
5) Apéri, Voláda, Óthos, Pylés
6) Ammoopí
7) Airport
8) Afiártis beaches
9) Vróntis

For more information about the exact times and bus fares, contact:
- 2245022338 and
- ktelkarpathou@gmail.com

Taxi

Kárpathos has eighteen taxis for the visitors, based at a very central point of Pigádia.

Radio taxi tel.: 2245022705.

There is a table put up at the taxi rank that informs the visitors about the fare to the most common destinations. In case you want to get to the airport, you had better make a reservation in advance!

DISTANCE

	PIGADIA	AIRPORT	AMMOOPI	APELLA	APERI	ARKASA	AVLONA	AFIARTIS	VOLADA	DIAFANI
PIGADIA		16	8	20	8	16	52	12	10	53
AIRPORT	16		10	36	24	10	68	1	26	69
AMMOOPI	8	10		28	16		60	9	18	61
APELLA	20	36	28		11	26	32	35	12	34
APERI	8	24	16	11		16	39	23	2	41
ARKASA	16	10		26	16		51	9	14	53
AVLONA	52	68	60	32	39	51		67	40	8
AFIARTIS	12	1	9	35	23	9	67		25	68
VOLADA	10	26	18	12	2	14	40	25		42
DIAFANI	53	69	61	34	41	53	8	68	42	
KYRA PANAGIA	10	26	18	14	8	22	42	25	8	44
LASTOS	16	32	24	16	7	18	44	31	5	46
LEFKOS	33	31	31	15	26	18	33	30	23	35
MENETES	8	12	5	25	15	7	53	11	15	55
MESOCHORI	29	37	33	13	21	23	31	36	21	33
OTHOS	12	28	17	14	4	13	42	27	2	43
OLYMPOS	48	64	56	28	35	47	6	63	36	6
PYLES	14	20	15	17	7	9	45	19	5	47
SPOA	26	42	34	9	16	28	25	41	17	27
FOINIKI	18	12	15	24	14	2	49	11	13	51

GETTING AROUND

A journey in the Aegean sea

IN KILOMETRE

KYRA PANAGIA	LASTOS	LEFKOS	MENETES	MESOCHORI	OTHOS	OLYMPOS	PYLES	SPOA	FOINIKI	
10	16	33	8	29	12	48	14	26	18	PIGADIA
26	32	31	12	37	28	64	20	42	12	AIRPORT
18	24	31	5	33	17	56	15	34	15	AMMOOPI
14	16	15	25	13	14	28	17	9	24	APELLA
8	7	26	15	21	4	35	7	16	14	APERI
22	18	18	7	23	13	47	9	28	2	ARKASA
42	44	33	53	31	42	6	45	25	49	AVLONA
25	31	30	11	36	27	63	19	41	11	AFIARTIS
8	5	23	15	21	2	36	5	17	13	VOLADA
44	46	35	55	33	43	6	47	27	51	DIAFANI
	13	25	24	23	10	38	13	18	21	KYRA PANAGIA
13		28	20	25	6	40	9	21	17	LASTOS
25	28		27	6	20	29	17	10	16	LEFKOS
21	20	27		32	10	49	10	30	11	MENETES
23	25	6	32		23	27	22	8	22	MESOCHORI
10	6	20	10	23		37	3	18	11	OTHOS
38	40	29	49	27	37		41	21	45	OLYMPOS
13	9	17	10	22	3	41		22	8	PYLES
18	21	10	30	8	18	21	22		26	SPOA
21	17	16	11	22	11	45	8	26		FOINIKI

Rented Cars

Rental outlets on the island offer a great number of cars, motorbikes, scooters and ATVs at a wide range of prices and meet all tastes. You can find them at specific points of the island but their people are eager to serve you wherever you are. The size of the island and the large number of destinations make the car necessary for the exploration of the wonderful island.

- SOFIA'S CAR RENTAL (Arkása) 2245061465
- EUROMOTO (Afoti, Pigádia) 2245023238
- AUTOLAND (Pigádia) 2245029167
- AUTOTOUR (Afoti, Pigádia) 2245022702
- BUDGET (Airport) 2245023873
- TAKIS RENT A CAR (Afoti, Pigádia) 6979495545
- CHEAP CARS (Airport) 6980015535
- UNITED KARPATHOS (Arkása) 2245061116
- SAINT NICHOLAS BEACH (Arkása) 2245061360
- ENTERPRISE (Airport) 2245091310
- THRIFTY (Pigádia) 2245029051
- MARGARITA (Pigádia) 2245022375
- SIXT (Pigádia) 2245023300
- AVIS (Pigádia & Airport) 2245091323
- UNITED CAR RENTAL (Arkása) 6972159405
- EXPLORE (Pigádia) 2245029059
- ALPHA (Arkása) 2245061352
- AMMOOPI RENTAL (Ammoopí) 224508115
- AVIS (Pigádia) 2245022702
- AUTOUNION (Afoti, Pigádia) 2245023703
- BRAVO (Pigádia) 2245022916
- HRONIS (Ammoopí) 6974133819
- LEFKOS (Káto Lefkós) 6977918774
- SUPERBIKES (Pigádia) 6987270285
- AUTOMOTO KARPATHOS (Pigádia) 2245022048
- BRAVO (Pigádia) 2245022916
- HRONIS (Ammoopí) 6974133819
- LEFKOS (Káto Lefkós) 6977918774
- SUPERBIKES (Pigádia) 6987270285
- AUTOMOTO KARPATHOS (Pigádia) 2245022048

Sea Tours

There are several vessels, many of them offering food, music and tour guides, that can take you to the remote and inaccessible beaches of the island but also to Diafáni, the island of Saría, Trístomo and Vroukoúnta. You can also privately hire a boat following contact with the travel agency. The boats leave from the ports of Pigádia and Diafáni. Here are the boats certified by the Port Authorities of Kárpathos, although there are many more vessels to hire:

- CHRYSOVALANTOU III 6978870741
- KONSTANTINOS M 6980162657
- CAP. NIKOLAS 6977987008
- SOFIA MY LOVE 6978595293

"Captain Manólis" will take you to north Kárpathos and Saría

HISTORY

Mythology

According to mythology, the first inhabitant of the island was the Titan Iapetós, son of Ouranós and Gaía (Earth) and brother of the formidable Krónos, the father of Días (Zeus). The son of Iapetós and his wife Asia was the famous Promithéas, the man who stole the fire from the gods and gave it to humans. It has also been reported that Kárpathos used to be the place where all Titans had been living before the great Titan War, which ended with the victory and dominance of the Olympian gods.

Lithograph depicting the Giants capturing god 'Aris

Apart from the Titans, the island was also inhabited by the mythical Giants, the most recognizable of them being Efiáltis, who, together with his brother Ótos, both sons of Poseidon, arrested and captured the god of war, Aris! The name of Afiártis is supposedly a corruption of the mythical giant's name. The myth says that apart from the Titans and the Giants the island was also inhabited by the Telchínes, the first semi-god craftsmen, who processed iron and copper. The strikingly wild and unique landscape of the island is perhaps the reason why Ancient Greeks considered Kárpathos home of the most amazing creatures of Greek Mythology.

The Name of the Island

The origin of the word Kárpathos has not fully been clarified yet. The two prevailing versions is that the island was named after the plant *kárpasos* that flourished here especially in antiquity (the same applies to the peninsula of Karpasía of Cyprus) or -according to mythology- that the locals abducted the Olympian gods and brought them to the island and, therefore, they were called Arpátheoi (from *arpázo* meaning grab and *theoí* meaning gods in Greek). The word was later corrupted and became Karpátheoi and finally Karpáthioi (meaning Karpathians). Homer reports the island as Krápathos. In ancient historic years, the island is also reported as Tetrápolis (meaning four towns) due to its four mighty towns. The name Anemóessa (meaning full of winds), a name frequently attributed to all the Aegean Islands due to the strong winds blowing in the archipelago, was also given to Kárpathos. In the medieval Frank period, it was named Skarpánto and that was the name the Italians also used during their occupation of the Dodecanese in the early 20th century. In Ottoman years, it was called Kerpé.

Prehistoric Period - Neolithic Period - Copper Age (4000 - 1000 BC)

According to excavation findings, Kárpathos has been inhabited at least since 4000 BC. The Carians (pre-Hellenic tribe from SW Asia Minor) must have been the first inhabitants. Recent excavations to the south of the island have brought to light a settlement from the Late Neolithic period, which reveals traces of continuous habitation until the Early Copper Age (1800 BC). The finds include mainly agricultural tools (millstones, mortars as well as axes and blades from obsidian of Mílos) and bones of domestic animals. It becomes obvious that there was systematic wheat culture and an early form of trade. Just think we are talking about 6000 years ago! At London Museum there is a statuette of the Neolithic period found here that dates back to between 4500 and 3200 BC! There are also remarkable finds related to the natural history of the island, such as fossil traces of rhinos and deer dating back to dozens of thousands years ago! Towards the late 3rd millennium BC the entire Aegean starts suffering from extensive turmoil. Settlements are abandoned, new ones are built, fortifications are constructed, the burial habits change and commerce is reduced, while the appearance of new architectural and pottery types is interpreted by several scholars as an indication of the arrival of new populations. It is the period of the Minoan civilization of Crete, which dramatically affected the entire Greek archipelago, including neighbouring

Kárpathos! The ancient historian Diodorus Siculus reports that the famous King Minos of Crete sent colonists to the island in the period known as Minoan Thalassocracy (1700 - 1450 BC). The main settlement of the time must have been Pigádia, according to finds from the north side of the bay (Vróntis), while excavations have also brought to light two country houses in the area of Afiártis dating back to 1700 BC. The tremendous explosion of the volcano of Santoríni took place circa 1650 BC and it was possibly the start of the decline of the Minoan civilization. A new Hellenic tribe arrives at that point, the Achaeans, who start out from the area of Árgos of the Peloponnese under the leadership of Ioklós, son of Dimoléon, in order to colonize the island. Now it was the turn of Mycenae to dominate Greece! In his Iliad, Homer informs us that Kárpathos participated in the Trojan War with ships (circa 1100 BC) under the orders of Feídippos and Ántifos.

Geometric and Archaic Periods (1000 - 500 BC)

Kárpathos followed all the phases of Greek history and, as a result, it was also occupied and inhabited by the last Greek tribe, the Dorians, who mainly came from the Greek mainland and built four significant towns, the so-called *Tetrápolis* of Kárpathos, according to Strabo. The confederation of towns was a typical Dorian feature and included Potídaion or Poseídion (Pigádia), Arkeseía (Arkása), Vroukoúnta (to the north of Olympos) and Nísyros (possibly in the little island of Saría, although it has not been identified yet). The island achieved great prosperity during the Dorian occupation, as proven by the numerous finds and inscriptions from excavations in the three of the four towns. The common point of reference in Dorian confederations was always a temple. Kárpathos, although an island of Poseidon, must have accommodated the temple of Lindía Athená at Potídaion.

Classical Period (500 - 336 BC)

In the classical years of the ancient Greek history, Kárpathos continued thriving and, according to reports of ancient Greek historians and excavation finds, the towns were full of magnificent buildings, such as temples of Aphrodite, the Dióscuri, etc.

Coins of Karpathos depicting dolphins, Poseidon's symbol

Coins were also minted, while the silver staters depicting dolphins were the registered trademarks of Poseidon's cult. The Tetrápolis of Kárpathos must not have had any involvement in the Persian Wars, although it became a member of the Delian League in 477 BC, which aimed at defending Greece and taking revenge on the Persians. The island belonged to the region of Caria, together with the south Dodecanese and SW Asia Minor, and contributed an annual amount to the league. Not before long, the alliance came under the strict Athenian rule and triggered the civil Peloponnesian War that burst out among Athens, Sparta and their allies in 431 BC. Although a Dorian colony, Kárpathos took sides with Athens. This is also inferred from the vote of gratitude the demos of Athens took in favour of the people of Kárpathos in 406 BC. The reason for the vote was a big cypress cut from the garden of Apollo in the verdant area of Píni, to the north of Voláda, which had been donated by the Karpathians to Athens for the reconstruction of the temple of Poliás Athena in the Acropolis of Athens. In 404 BC the Spartans occupied Kárpathos but the Athenians took it back in 397 BC under the leadership of Kónon, who granted full independence to the island.

Hellenistic Period
(336 BC – 42 BC)

After the death of Alexander the Great and during the competition among his successors, Kárpathos was found in the eye of the storm. When Dimítrios Poliorkitís, one of the successors, was defeated by the Rhodians in Rhodes in 304 BC, the island was submitted to the Rhodian state and came under its great influence, particularly from the city of Líndos, in almost all aspects of life. Potídaion was the town that really flourished in that period. Thanks to its powerful navy, Rhodes remained autonomous throughout the Hellenistic period and, as a result, Kárpathos irrevocably connected its fate to Rhodes until it was captured by the Romans in the mid-1st c. AD.

Roman Period
(42 BC – 330 AD)

Shortly before the end of the millennium and after the state of Rhodes had considerably declined, the Romans captured Kárpathos. However, culture and trade must have th-

Dorian Resolution for Kárpathos

The inhabitants of Vroukoúnta decided to honour the physician Minókritos, son of Mitródoros from Sámos, who had offered the island free medical services for twenty years. They put forward a resolution through which they thanked the physician for his services, awarded him a laurel wreath, and granted him and his descendants the right to the Karpathian citizenship and the right to participate in the rituals and celebrations of the town. The resolution was inscribed on a marble column, which was positioned in the yard of the temple of Poseidon! The inscription is dated to the 2nd c. BC and is exhibited at the British Museum of London.

The inscription of the Dorian resolution at the London Museum

rived in that period as well, as evidenced by the inscriptions of the time, which praise and appreciate the Romans who relieved the island from the curse of piracy. Furthermore, the Romans reduced taxes and gave motives to the Karpathians. In the years of Emperor Diocle-

> **Lucullan Banquets!**
>
> The most famous gourmand of history, the Roman general Lucullus, used to send to Kárpathos a ship in order to fish the delicious parrotfish, which were famous already from antiquity and the emperor considered indispensable for his epical meals!

tian (245-313 AD), Kárpathos belonged to the Provincia insularum (province of the islands) of the Roman Empire, whose capital was Rhodes.

Icon depicting Agios Ioánnis the Karpathian

Byzantine Period (330 AD – 1204 AD)

From 330 AD onwards, in the years of Constantine I, the Roman Empire was fully Hellenized in the East due to racial and cultural relationships with the Greeks, whilst at the same time it maintained the name and the morals of Rome. The capital was transferred to Constantinople. In the years of Theodosius I (395 AD), the empire, including Kárpathos, adopts

The Early Christian basilica of Agia Foteiní at Pigádia

KARPATHOS

Christianity and the island is included in the administrative region of the islands. The most typical building of that period is the Early Christian basilica of Agia Foteiní, on the coast of Áfoti, very close to Pigádia, as well as Agia Anastasía in Arkása. According to the minutes of the Fifth Ecumenical Synod of Constantinople in 553 AD, Kárpathos was an autonomous seat of a Bishop, a title later held by Agios Ioánnis the Karpathian. In the 7th c. AD, subsequent invasions and pillages –mainly by Arabs, Persians and Saracens– made the locals retreat from the coasts and seek shelter in the mountains, in the interior of the island. This is the period when the current villages were built and Pigádia became a piratical base. The Karpathians are reported to have contributed two ships to the Byzantine fleet of Emperor Nikifóros Fokás in 961 AD, when he decided to chase away the Arabs, who had captured Crete. From then on, Kárpathos was included in the administrative region of Crete.

Frank Occupation (1204 AD - 1538 AD)

After almost one thousand years, the Orthodox Byzantine Empire started to decline and shrink before it finally surrendered to Catholic Frank Crusaders, who deviated from their course to the Holy Land during the Fourth Crusade and captured Constantinople on April 13, 1204. The entire Greek territory was fragmented into small kingdoms distributed to noblemen that had taken part in the crusade. Unlike in most of the Aegean islands, the Franks did not instantly arrive in Kárpathos because Léon Gavalás, a Byzantine official from Constantinople, had occupied the island together with Rhodes and

had been proclaimed *Árchon of Rhodes and Kárpathos and Caesar of South Sporádes* in the name of the Byzantine emperor. Gavalás helped the islands develop, minted coins, and fought against the Venetian Marco Sanudo, who had established the Duchy of the Archipelago in the Cyclades, and the Greek emperor of Níkaia (Asia Minor), Ioannis Vatátzis. However, he managed to maintain the island's independence. In 1240, he was succeeded by his brother, Ioánnis Gavalás, who at first allied with the Greek Empire of Níkaia before his territory was finally annexed to the empire in 1248. Although the Empire of Níkaia finally recaptured Constantinople in 1261, it lost Kárpathos to the Genoese in 1282. The brothers Andrea and Ludovico Moresco became the sovereigns of the island, which was ceded to them together with Rhodes and Kásos by the Byzantine emperor as a reward for the services they had offered him.

Digenís

According to the popular tradition of the island, the two carved tombs that have been found at Kourí, near the village of Voláda, belong to the mythical Digenís Akrítas and his wife. Digenís was a legendary hero who guarded the borders of medieval Greece

The "Palaiókastro" between Apéri and Voláda

Their domination lasted until 1306, when the island came under the Venetian Andrea Cornaro from Crete. After a period in which the Morescos wanted to recapture the island and the four-year occupation by the Ioannite Knights of Rhodes, Kárpathos was once again occupied by the Cornaros in 1316. The Cornaros were an aristocratic family of Venice who had become sovereigns in the Peloponnese, Euboea, Cyprus, Crete and Dalmatia. Four of them held senior positions in Venice and finally rose to the supreme office of the Doge of the Most Serene Republic of Venice. In Kárpathos they built lots of fortifications and churches. Continuous wars and piracy had dramatically reduced the population of the island at the time. It is reported that only 300 people were living in Kárpathos in 1470! The domination of the Cornaro family in Kárpathos finished in 1538, during the war between Venice and Turkey, when the Ottoman Turks landed on the island under the leadership of the notorious pirate Hayreddin Barbarossa.

Turkish Occupation (1538 AD - 1911 AD)

The Turks were never really interested in the island and never settled here. Kárpathos was under the Ottoman bey of Rhodes, who used to send a number of officers once in a while in order to collect the taxes for the sultan. However, the real governors of the island were the *dimogerontía* (the elderly) and the *proestoí* (a type of self-government consisting of the most eminent and richest citizens). Piracy was a serious menace to Kárpathos, particularly in the 16th c., when things became really bad for the locals. Trístomo and Saría were notorious piratical dens, while Arkása was converted into a real slave market!

The Greek Revolution of 1821 against the Turkish yoke burst out in Greek mainland on March 25, while one

HISTORY

Ships like that used to dock at Trístomo
during the 1821 Greek War of Independence

HISTORY

Raised flags at Menetés on the anniversary of October 5

month later, the extremely active and efficient seamen of the neighbouring island of Kásos encouraged the Karpathians to enter the common national struggle. As a result, the flag of the revolted Greeks was enthusiastically raised in Kárpathos on May 4, 1821. All the people of Kárpathos helped in every possible way the just fight for independence. Trístomo, the former piratical den, is now a base of the Greek fleet, a shipyard is created on the coast of Kyrá Panagiá, the men become sailors, the church melts the oblations in order to offer the valuable metal, and the wealthiest citizens offer money to the national struggle. In 1823, Kárpathos proclaims the union with the revolted Greece and is included in the province of Santorini. The Greeks, following a tough struggle of almost 10 years, become independent, but by virtue of the 1830 London Protocol, which confirmed the independence of Greece, the Great Powers decided that the Dodecanese, including Kárpathos, should not be included in the newly established Greek State and should remain under the rule of the Turk sultan. There was great disappointment. Expostulatory letters that could help things change were sent in all directions but without any good results for the poor Karpathians, who saw that their long fight had been in vain and that they had to return to the domination of those whom they had chased out of their island.

The heavy taxes that were imposed by the Sublime Port of the sultan in 1870 led a great part of the population to gradually migrate to Greece and later to the USA.

Italian Occupation and Liberation (1912 AD – 1947 AD)

In 1911, Italy is involved in a war against the Ottoman Empire over Libya. The Italian fleet creates a diversion by occupying the Dodecanese, while a part of the Italian army and navy arrives in Kárpathos on May 12, 1912. Italy was supposed to return the islands immediately after the end of the war with Turkey but the Italian occupation was consolidated due to the Balkan Wars of 1912-1913 and World War I of 1914-1918. The same happened after 1918 as well, when Italy agreed with Greece, which in the meanwhile had liberated all the Aegean Islands from the Turks during the Balkan Wars, to cede the islands (except Rhodes), but the Greco-Turkish War of Asia Minor in 1919-1922 prevented the union with Greece and Italy broke the promise to the Greek government. On August 6, 1923, after the fascist party of Benito Mussolini had risen to power, Italy annexed the islands as a possession of the Italian Parliament in the name of King Victor Emmanuel. The building today accommodating the provincial authorities of Kárpathos, a typical example of the Italian colonial architecture, was the Italian command post. At first, the relationships of the locals with the Italian officers and soldiers were very good. However, the closer World War II got, the more oppressive the fascist regime of Mussolini became. After 1937, the Italian occupation became intolerable, while the Greek language and the Greek history were banned from schools, the possession of Greek flags and symbols was forbidden, and all the people should necessarily speak Italian. Things became worse when the Greco-Italian War burst out on October 28, 1940. Many Karpathians were recruited as volunteers in the Regiment of the Dodecanese that joined the Greek army in the Albanian front. The Italians were defeated in World War II and surrendered in 1943 but did not walk out of the Dodecanese. The Germans, who had been their allies until then, hastened to settle on the islands in case the divided Italian forces wanted to join the allies. However, as the Germans were also retreating from all European fronts, they also left Kárpathos on October 4, 1944. The Italians remained but the Karpathians could

Monument commemorating the revolt of the island against Italy in 1944

KARPATHOS | 31

HISTORY

The bust of C. Lítos at the square of the provincial building at Pigádia

not stand the Italian occupation anymore. The day after the German exit, on October 5, 1944, the men of the village of Menetés revolted, disarmed and captured the Italian guard (the imposing monument on the hill opposite Menetés is dedicated to that revolt). They were immediately followed by the inhabitants of Arkása and the rest of the villages. After one week the entire island was free. It was then that they informed the exiled Greek government, which was based in Egypt, about the declaration of the union with Greece. Seven brave young men sailed from Foiníki on a small boat called Imakoláta and after five days they reached Alexandria of Egypt, where they met the Greek government and the allies. They returned after a few days aboard two allied destroyers. At the little port of Foiníki there is a monument commemorative of the heroic journey. Kárpathos together with the rest of the Dodecanese were not immediately given to Greece as the British remained on the island for a few more years before the Greek flag was finally raised in Kárpathos on March 31, 1947, after the Treaty of Paris was signed. The official celebration of the union with Greece took place one year later, on March 7, 1948. This is the date the incorporation of the Dodecanese is officially celebrated, while October 5 is the local celebration in Kárpathos (and mainly in Menetés).

The Heroes of Kárpathos

Two are the most eminent Karpathians whose names have been written with gold letters in the recent history of the island of World War II. The first is the squadron leader Panagiótis Orfanídis from Apéri, who was killed during the Greco-Italian War of 1940 together with three other officers when his airplane crashed while bombing Italian targets in the Albanian front. His bust adorns the yard of the cathedral at Apéri. The second is Christóforos Lítos from Voláda. Lítos was a passionate patriot who escaped from Kárpathos in 1938 so as not to be arrested by the Italians because he had helped some convicts break away. In 1940, he joined the Regiment of the Dodecanese without hesitation in order to fight in the Albanian front. Because he was a very capable person, he was transferred to Crete, where he was trained in espionage and sabotage. He fought very bravely in the legendary Battle of Crete and then left for the Middle East before he secretly returned to Kárpathos in 1943. He remained hidden in the mountains for 6 months spying the Italian and German troops for the account of the allies. Lítos was decorated by both the Greek and the British governments. After the liberation, he returned to his beloved Kárpathos but fate played a dirty trick on him. Although he had escaped death so many times during the war, he was destined to have a tragic end when he stepped on a mine at Vróntis Beach, outside Pigádia, in 1945. His busts adorn his birthplace, Voláda, the square of the provincial building in Pigádia, as well as the point where he lost his life at the beach of Vróntis.

FOLKLORE CULTURE

There are so many things to include in this chapter! The folklore tradition of Kárpathos is among the richest in Greece. The famous village of Olympos is a folklore museum on its own! Although Kárpathos is not particularly big, every village has its own character with regard to traditional costumes, architecture and morals. There are four folklore museums in the village. However, in my opinion, the most important element of Kárpathos in this chapter is its inhabitants, whose love has maintained the traditions of their island alive in all aspects of social activity. I was happy to see that in almost all the houses I visited (even newly built) there is a corner dedicated to tradition, which honours the origins, the morals and the customs of the island.

Traditional Costumes

The men's costume consists of the *vráka*, that is, long and loose-fitting blue trousers, a version of which is worn in most Aegean Islands, completed by the *zipoúni*, a slack dark cotton shirt, which is tied on the *vráka* with the help of *mizóro*, a woolen knitted waistband. The *stavroperíko*, a double-breasted waistcoat with rich embroidery, is worn over the shirt. The shoes are called *stivánia*, which are boots from goatskin up to the knees with soles made from swine skin. In Olympos there are still traditional craftsmen making *stivánia*! Finally, the head is covered with the *toutouziótiko*, a black cloth cap (for most of the inhabitants) or a red fez with a tassel (for the most eminent ones).

The women's costume is, of course, much more elaborately adorned, with strong influences from Byzantine clothes. The traditional costume includes the white cotton shirt with the loose sleeves, which are embellished with beautiful embroidery worked with silk thread. The lower part of the body is covered by the external dress, which is adorned with folds and silk ribbons and usually forms one piece with the *panokórmi* (meaning upper body), which is worn under the shirt. I say usually because the women of Olympos instead of the dress wear the fa-

Philosophical...inscription of 1910 at the square of Olympos

mous *kavádi*, a long dark cloth, open on the front or on the sides and adorned with beautiful embroidery patterns. If the woman is young and single, she wears the *sakofoústano*, while if she is older and married, she usually wears the *kavádi*. The *podiá* (apron) is worn over the dress or the *kavádi*. Women also wear *stivánia*. Around their head they wrap a *mantíla* or *tsempéri*, whose colour varies depending on the marital status of the woman: black for married and white for single women, though always adorned with colourful flowers –a rather symbolic feature.

The famous soufás (ARKASA)

In celebrations, weddings and other official social events the woman's costume is embellished with additional items. A ribbon with gold coins is tied around the head, while various jewels are hung in their chest, such as the *manákia* (siver necklace), the *mertzána* (coral jewel), and the *klónes* (pearls). A necessary accessory is *kolaínes*, a necklace with gold liras indicating the financial status of the girl's family. Finally, instead of *stivánia* they wear red slippers with gold embroidery. As it has already been mentioned, the costume may vary a little from village to village. For example, the woman's costume in south Kárpathos is called *Vésta* and does not include the *kavádi*, while a second *tsempéri* is wrapped around the head. This costume is also called *katohorítiki* (meaning of the south island). In any case, you do not have to visit a folklore museum in order to see a woman's costume as you are bound to see women of Olympos wearing costumes while walking down the street!

The Traditional House of Kárpathos and Architecture

In the chapter with the history of the island it was reported that in the Middle Ages, due to piratical raids, the locals left the coasts and moved to more mountainous and inaccessible areas, often invisible from the sea, that is, to the locations of the current villages of Kárpathos. They built their houses from stone and wood and made small windows. The houses usually had two floors and were very close to each other. White is not the prevailing colour as it happens in the Cyclades and other Aegean Islands. The houses are colourful and they often have an elaborate gypsum decoration. The double-headed eagles usually found on the rails of the balconies of Olympos reveal the influence the Greek Byzantine Empire had on the inhabitants in medieval years. The roof of the house was supported by a large wooden beam,

Decorated house (ARKASA)

Railing with the double-headed eagle of the Byzantine Empire (Olympos)

the *mesá*, which was in turn supported by a vertical and thick cylindrical post at the centre of the house. Each floor was about two metres high. The two floors communicated through an external staircase, while there was always a paved yard with at least one tree planted at the centre. The front door is divided horizontally into the *panopórti* (upper door) and the *katopórti* (lower door). The upper floor usually included a *soufás*, the traditional bed of Kárpathos, and the lower floor the fireplace, the kitchen or

Exterior of house in Menetés

Oil painting depicting locals dancing (cafe in Voláda)

the internal walls of the house had several rows of shelves, where plates and utensils rested. Valuable woven items and rugs of the family hang from the little rails of *soufás*, while the vertical post was also particularly adorned with embroidered fabrics. As you can realize by yourselves, the *soufás* of the Karpathian house is the apotheosis of popular art!

Music and Dancing

The musical instruments mainly used by the Karpathians in feasts and celebrations are also traditional. First and foremost, the Karpathian *lýra* (lyre) with its bow, then the *laoúto* (traditional instrument with strings), and finally the *tsamboúna* (bagpipe with a wooden pipe and a bag of goat hide). The violin is also quite common. The Karpathian music and songs are strongly influenced by neighbouring Crete. The best musicians of the island come from the village of Menetés. The *syrmatiká* songs are gentle melodious ballads lauding love and nature but also mourning the homesickness of migrants. Another kind of song is the *mantináda*, the traditional 15-syllable rhyming jolly couplet of Crete in fast tempo. Most of the times the verses are im-

kéllos, as it is called in Olympos, and certainly a *soufás*. The *soufás*, the most typical item of the traditional house of Kárpathos, which is still constructed in almost all contemporary Karpathian houses, is a wooden structure fully fitted between the two walls, with two levels and a few steps. It consists of the *panosoúfi* (upper), the space where the children of the family used to sleep, while, if there was a baby, it slept in a hanging swing-hammock above the *panosoúfi*. The couple slept in the lower part, the *katosoúfi*, which is also elevated and protected by the *trapouzánia*, which were wood-carved little rails. All the whitewashed surfaces and spaces under the *soufás*, or *apokrýatos*, are used for storing the provisions of the family. Vertically to the *soufás* there were *págkes*, which were wide and embellished couches for relaxation. The latter were also used for storing foodstuffs inside them. All around,

> "...My dear Arkása and Menetés,
> Foiníki and Pigádia,
> You are so far away from me
> and life is so much empty.
> Voláda, Óthos and Pylés,
> and you, my pretty Apéri,
> Oh, how much I miss you now
> only my heart can tell it!
> Spóa, Diafáni, Olympos,
> beautiful Mesochóri,
> I hurt because your mountains
> and I are not together!"

KARPATHOS | 37

Young women from Olympos wearing traditional costumes
(photo: Eirini Balaská)

promptu invented and they often have satirical content. Finally, there is the famous *moirológi* (lament). However, there are also the *patinádes*, love ballads sung in the street by a lovesick man, similar to the serenades of the Ionian Islands. Two are the most important local dances: *páno horós*, which is quick and jovial, and *káto horós*, which accompanies *syrmatiká* songs. There are also some other dances as well but they are rather rare, such as *zervós* (meaning left in Greek), which is danced in a direction opposite to the usual.

Morals and Customs

Kanakariá. The most typical moral / custom of Kárpathos, which will certainly fascinate you, has to do with family structure and the past social organization of Kárpathos. The male kanakáris or the female kanakárissa was the first-born child of a family, which inherited the entire property of the parents. Kanakáris was named after his father's father and inherited all the property of the father, while kanakárissa was named after her mother's mother and inherited all the property of the mother. The rest of the children had no rights over the family property! The property was inherited after the wedding of the first-born boy or girl. The parents kept for themselves a small part of the property, the so-called gerontomíri, in order to have some income. In case one of the spouses died and the couple had no children, the surviving member should return the property to the deceased spouse's parents. The custom had also social effects. For example, the cathedral of Olympos –Koímisi tis Theotókou– was intended only for first-born boys, while the rest attended the service in other churches. The customary law of inheritance was abolished through an official decree of the Italian authorities in 1922. It is obvious that it aimed at the control and retention of family property.

The wedding. It is only natural that this important event has been affected by the particular folklore characteristics of the people of Kárpathos. A three-day celebration is held in Olympos when two people get married! Buns and other cookies that will be offered to the guests are prepared on the eve of the wedding, while the clothes and other household items of the bride are exhibited in her house. At the same time, musicians walk around the village playing and singing, in this way inviting all the inhabitants to the event and the celebration of the following day. On the wedding day, the musicians go to the houses of the bridegroom and the bride and accompany them to the church where the sacramental rite will take place. A traditional banquet follows with lots of food, wine and dancing. The following day is dedicated to the custom of antigámos (counter-wedding)! The musicians accompany the best man from his house to the house of the bride, where a new celebration takes place!

Eftá (seven). It takes place seven days after the birth of a child. The relatives and friends of the couple gather in order to wish the newborn child while singing mantinádes and offering presents. The mother treats them to a sweet especially made for that moment, the alevrás, which contains flour, butter and honey.

Celebrations

The religious feeling of the Karpathians is very deep and the combination with their cheerful insular nature, which is always ready for revelling, singing and dancing, leads to local religious celebrations! In Kárpathos there are a large number of feasts, villages and country churches! In most of them, the service is followed by revelry with lots of food, dancing and singing. You do not have to worry about the period you should visit the island because religious celebrations are held throughout the year. It is a really beautiful picture when you see pilgrims from all other villages arriving on their donkeys, whose back is adorned with colourful blankets. The most famous celebrations in calendar order (the most important are underlined) are as follows:

- **February 2:**
Ypapantí. Arkása

- **February 10:**
Agios Harálambos, Apéri

- **March 25:**
Evangelismós tis Theotókou
(Annunciation of the Virgin), Pigádia

- **April 23:**
Agios Geórgios (St. George).
Páno Lefkós, Foiníki, Church of Vassón

- **May 5:** Agia Eiríni. Mesochóri

- **June 30:**
Agioi Apóstoloi (the Apostles), Pigádia

- **July 7:** Agia Kyriakí.
At the namesake church and location, near Pigádia

- **July 7:** Agia Marina, Lástos

- **July 26:** Agia Paraskeví, Pylés

- **July 27:**
Agios Panteleímon. Stes, Katódio

- **August 6:** Metamorphosis
(the Transfiguration)
Diafáni, Menetés, Óthos, Apéri.

- **August 10:**
Chrysovalántou. Olympos

- **August 15:** Koímisi tis Theotókou
(the Dormition). Olympos, Menetés, Apéri, Pylés

- **August 23:** Enniámera Panagías
(nine days after the Dormition). Kyrá Panagiá, Mertónas

- **August 29:**
Agios Ioannis. Vroukoúnta

- **September 5:**
Agios Zaharías. Saría

- **September 7:**
The Virgin's Birthday.
Larniótissa of Pigádia

- **September 8:**
The Virgin's Birthday.
Mesochóri, Voláda

- **September 14:**
Timíou Stavroú
(Raising of the Holy Cross), Pylés

- **September 17:** Agia Sofia. Arkása

- **October 8:** Agia Pelagía. Spóa

- **October 18:** Agios Loukás. Ápella

FOLKLORE – CULTURE

- **November 8:**
  Taxiárches (Archangels). Lástos

- **November 3:**
  Agios Geórgios Methystís. Spóa, Pigádia, Óthos (the sealed barrels with the new wine are opened)

- **November 21:**
  Eisódia Theotókou (Presentation of Mary). Apéri (the cathedral of Kárpathos)

- **December 6:**
  Agios Nikólaos, Foiníki

Great celebration at Agia Marina of Lástos on July 17

Cultural Events

Apart from private celebrations and religious feasts, several other cultural events are organized in the summer by the Municipality of Kárpathos and the very active cultural organization KOPAP (Karpathian Organization for Culture, Sports and Education). Exhibitions, theatrical performances and concerts are held at the open-air Poseidónio amphitheatre at the beach of Pigádia. The championship of skandalópetra (free diving without gear) is also held at the same beach. A very popular event is the local football championship held every summer with the participation of teams from all the villages.

There are two radio stations on the island: Radio Olympos at 100.5 for the north part and the Municipal Radio Station of Kárpathos at 101.3 FM for the rest of the island.

A journey in the Aegean sea

ECONOMY

The economy of the island is mainly based on tourism, which has rapidly been developing in recent years. There are over 200 tourist units (hotels, rooms and apartments) on the island, with approximately 7,000 beds available. Together with accommodation and entertainment facilities, they provide employment to most of the professionally active locals. Agriculture is not particularly developed in Kárpathos due to the mountainous terrain. However, fruit and vegetables are cultivated mainly to the south of the island, especially in the area Kípos tou Afiárti (Garden of Afiártis), while cereals are farmed in the rural settlement of Avlóna to the north. Extensive areas in many parts of the island are covered with

Viniculture is a main contributor in primary production in Karpathos

olive trees. Stock breeding is the main contributor to primary production. More than 12,000 goats and sheep are farmed in the grasslands of the island and there is even a dairy unit making milk products. Apiculture also holds a prominent position, with almost 6,000 hives producing top quality honey (mainly thyme). As in any island, the locals like fishing and there are approximately 100 professional and amateur fishing boats.

Stock-breeding is one of the basic occupations

THE SETTLEMENTS

Despite its small size, Kárpathos has several settlements, sixteen of them being the most important. Below, they are presented in alphabetical order.

Ammoopí

A coastal tourist resort within 8 km from Pigádia and 8 km from the airport, whose name means "a hole in the sand." Due to the great number of tourists, there are about 100 permanent inhabitants. Numerous tourist units operate in the area as well as restaurants and mini markets. Here you can find some of the best and most famous beaches of the island with wonderful waters, such as Mikrí (small) Ammoopí and Megáli (large) Ammoopí, Votsalákia and Kastélia, all of them organized. The lacy coastline and the relief of the ground have split the local shore into smaller sections, such as Lakkí, Fokiá, Kastélia, Péra Ámmos and a few others, but at the same time they have made it one of the most cosmopolitan destinations on the island.

The beach of Megáli Ammoopí

Panoramic view of Apéri

Apéri

The old capital of the island until 1892 as indicated by its name, which is a corrupted form of the word apérgi meaning capital. Today it accommodates the cathedral of Kárpathos and Kásos, the church of Panagía (the Virgin) and the building for the offices of the cathedral, which dominate the north part of the ravine. It was built in the medieval years and is invisible from the sea for the fear of pirates. The village is situated at an altitude of 320m and is built around a verdant ravine. Approximately 500 people live here. The noble style

The little church and the plane tree at the centre of Apéri

The Early Christian basilica of Agia Anastasia and the little church of Agia Sofia

of the houses witnesses the glorious past of a large village. Under the pretty little bridge of the ravine, which connects the seven quarters of the village, there is a spring with cool water next to a beautiful plane tree and the church of Agios Nikólaos and Agia Anna. The cultural society of the village is called Omónoia (concord) and is very active. In the village there are cafes and taverns. It is within 8 km from Pigádia and 20 km from the airport. The verdant locations and springs of Katódio and Mertónas as well as the famous beach of Kyrá Panagiá belong to Apéri.

Arkása

The village is the current descendant of ancient Arkeseía, one of the four powerful towns of the island. It has uninterruptedly been inhabited at least since the Mycenaean period (12th c. BC). Approximately 600 people live today in the village. The landmark of the area is the steep Cape Paliókastro, on top of which stands a fortified castle. The privileged location on the west side of the island made it the most important gate mainly to Crete. At the foot of Paliókastro you can admire the amazing Early Christian basilica of Agia Anastasía with the wonderful mosaic. As it happens in Apéri, a narrow dry river divides the quarters of the village, which accommodates a great number of hotels and the pretty sandy beach of Agios Nikólaos on its margins. Several taverns, restaurants and shops meet the needs of the visitors. There is also a museum in the village. Arkása is within 6 km from Pigádia and 10 km from the airport.

THE SETTLEMENTS

Panoramic view of Arkása with the Palaiókastro

THE SETTLEMENTS

THE SETTLEMENTS

The rural settlement on the plateau of Avlóna

Avlóna

Avlóna is a rural settlement built by the inhabitants of Olympos that has always served as the breadbasket of the famous village. In fact, there are no permanent inhabitants and the dozens of houses you can see only serve the needs of the farmers of Olympos. The stone country houses are called stávloi (stables). It is the northernmost settlement of the island and is built on a fertile plateau that produces top quality wine, fruit, vegetables and cereals. Avlóna is the end of the asphalt road. If you feel thirsty, you can find a canteen with refreshments here. The village is within 5 km from Olympos and 52 km from Pigádia.

Afiártis

Afiártis is not exactly a settlement but a vast area to the south of the island, extending from the foot of the mountain of Menetés called Kefálas to Cape Kastello, after the airport, which is the southernmost point of Kárpathos. This is the plain of the island, where the inhabitants of Menetés, to whom Afiártis belongs, maintain their vegetable gardens, especially in the area Kípos tou Afiárti. The area has greatly developed thanks to the large number of hotels and restaurants offering their services in the beautiful beaches, while the visitor can also find alternative tourism facilities, mainly windsur-

The impressive wreck at Cape Lígki

A journey in the Aegean sea

fing, in the beaches close to the airport as the winds are ideal for this sport, thus making Afiártis famous all over the world. At Cape Lígki, which is included in the military territory, there is a wreck visible (and highly photographed) from all the beaches of Afiártis, on the east coast. Approximately 30 people live permanently in the area.

Voláda

Voláda is within just 2 km after Apéri. It is built at an altitude of 450 m and is also invisible from the sea. Until 1815 it was the continuation of Apéri and they both formed a single settlement called Megálo Horió (big village). Approximately 350 people live in the village. Most of the houses are snow-white with red tiles on the roof and colourful windows. The beautiful picture is completed with narrow alleys with whitewashed steps, flower pots and a huge cross in the nearby hill, which is illuminated at night. It is the birthplace of the local hero of Kárpathos, Christóforos Lítos, whose bust adorns the main road. The church is dedicated to the patron saint of the village, Panagía Plagiá (the Virgin), and includes a miraculous icon made in 1791. Within a very short distance from the village, halfway from Apéri, you can visit the ruins of a medieval castle next to a pretty country church at the hill of Koráki. It is reported that the hill was already fortified in the Byzantine period, possibly already from antiquity. The highest mountain top of the island, Kalí Límni, with the beautiful plateau of Lástos, which you should by all means visit, as you should do with the verdant area of Piní with the flowing waters, belongs to the village of Voláda. In the village you can

The beaches of Limniá and Vathá at Afiártis is an attraction point for surfers

The beautiful Voláda on the slopes of Mt. Lástos

find taverns and cafes. The distance from Pigádia is 10 km and from the airport 26 km.

A forlorn woman of Olympos gazing at the sea at Diafáni
(by V. Hatzivassílis)

Diafáni

The asphalt road that connects Olympos with its port is 8 km long. Until a few years ago, when the asphalt connecting Pigádia with Olympos had not been completed, Olympos was almost exclusively served through the little port of Diafáni. It remains the second port of the island and liners still dock at its jetty. The village was named after someone called Diofánis, possibly a monk living in the area. Habitation dates back to ancient years but in recent years the settlement mainly developed after the end of World War II, when the Dodecanese was annexed to Greece. It is a pretty fishing village built along a pebbled beach, with se-

> When the Turkish authorities decided to separate Voláda from Apéri in 1815 and create two independent communities, the inhabitants, mainly of Voláda, strongly reacted under the village headman Michael Petrítis-Pnevmatikós. However, they did not manage to change the decision.

veral little taverns, cafes and accommodation facilities. The centre of the village is dominated by the church of Metamórfosis (the Transfiguration). The sculptures of the folk artist Hatzivassílis from Olympos, such as the fountain and the statue of the woman gazing at the sea, are particularly impressive. Small boats offer daily trips to the pretty coasts and beaches of the north part of the island, such as the nearby Vanánta, and the islet of Saría, Trístomo and Vroukoúnta. There are approximately 150 permanent inhabitants and Pigádia are 53 km away.

Lefkós

Lefkós serves Mesochóri as its port and source of tourist income. It is located to the NW of the island and has a population of 80 people. The village is divided into áno (upper) and káto (lower) Lefkós and is built in an idyllic location full of pines and successive coves that form magnificent lacy coasts. The islet off the coast is

The path that leads to the ruins of the Roman tank at Lefkós

called Sókastro (meaning inner castle) and, as indicated by its name, used to be a fortified position and a naval base of the Byzantine fleet. There are still some ruins of the Byzantine castle. The place has been inhabited since antiquity. At Riá

The golden sand of the beach of "Gialoú Choráfi" at Lefkós

The village of Menetés looks like an eyrie

there is a finely preserved tank of the Roman period, while in Áno Lefkós you can visit the 13th c. little church of Agios Geórgios. Lefkós is a summer resort with several hotels, rented rooms and country houses as well as taverns, cafes and shops. Above all, the village is famous for its magnificent beaches! The distance from Pigádia is 33 km.

Menetés

Menetés is the village of liberation and famous musicians! It is built at an altitude of 350 m and the view of the village is amazing from all directions! This is a really beautiful village! The houses are built on the slope of the hill of Profítis Ilías and face the opposite quarter on the holy rock, whose top is dominated by the impressive church of Panagía with the imposing bell tower at the paved square. The village was founded in medieval years by people from the coasts of Ammoopí and Afiártis so that they could be protected from pirates. As for the derivation of the name, according to a folk myth, a booming voice came from the sky ordering the people "Ménete, ménete!" (meaning stay here), when they decided to look for a new and safer place to live because they had been fed up with the pirates. The village has about 500 residents, including the areas of Afiártis and Ammoopí. Before reaching the village, you can admire at the top of a hill an impressive monument dedicated to the heroic revolt of October 5, 1944, when the people of Menetés chased off the Italian conquerors. Next to the holy rock, on the main road of the village, you can find the folklore museum. A few kilometres outside the village, along the road to Arkása, at Exíles, there is an 11th c. little church with an unusual shape, dedicated to Agios Mámmas. At Menetés you can find cafes and restaurants, while both

View of Menetés from the "Holy Rock"

Pigádia and the airport are at equal distances of 8 km from the village.

Mesochóri

This is one of the most picturesque villages of the island! Stuck on the steep cliffs of the NW coast, it looks at the open Karpathian Sea. It was built at this altitude (150 m above sea level) for the same reason that led the locals live in all non-coastal villages of the island: the pirates! On your way there, you can stop and enjoy a really amazing view of the village. Mesochóri is a rather small village with white houses with pebbled yards and narrow alleys, all full of pots and flowers. Park at the entrance of the village and continue on foot until the end of the road, in the square, at the brim of the cliff. The square is called skópi and, apart from the war memorial, you can also see two churches, Stavrós (The Holy Cross) and Agios Nikólaos. However, the pride of the village is the church of Panagía Vrysianí. In the yard there is a triple faucet with holy water. One of the greatest religious celebrations of the island is held here on September 8. Mesochóri is the olive producing area of Kárpathos. In the village you can find a tavern and a cafe. The population is approxima-

The view of Mesochóri from the road is spectacular

KARPATHOS

THE SETTLEMENTS

Óthos, the highest village of Karpathos *(photo: Karpathiakí newspaper)*

tely 350 people and the distance from Pigádia is 29 km.

Óthos

The village is built at an altitude of 510 m, on the slope of Mount Méloura, and is the highest inhabited point of the island, a few kilometres after Apéri and Voláda. It is named after the mythical Giant Ótos, the brother of Efiáltis, who lived here according to mythology. It was built in the 16th c. by people from the plain of Afiártis. Óthos is a small village that offers a wonderful view of the SE coasts of Kárpathos, especially if you sit in one of its little taverns in order to taste the famous local sausages. Most of the houses are painted indigo and their entrances are oriented to the east due to the strong west winds blowing in the area. Admire the church of Koímisi tis Theotókou (the Dormition) with the beautiful fountain. There is a folklore museum founded by the late researcher of local traditions and great lyre-player Kapsís! After a short while (almost 2 km), you get to Stes, the vegetable garden of Óthos. There are a few houses built in a breathtaking landscape with trees, vineyards, gardens and flowing waters. See the beautiful church of Agios Panteleímon and do not fail to enjoy the spectacular sunset! Óthos has a population of 350 people and lies within 12 km from Pigádia.

The idyllic "Stes"

A journey in the Aegean sea

Olympos

The most recognizable and famous village of Kárpathos and a breathing folklore museum! Although the phrase "Time has stopped here" may be heard as yet another cliché, Olympos is the place to prove its originality! The mountain on which the village is built used to be called Olympos in ancient times, just like the famous residence of the twelve gods of ancient Greece. The mountain is now called Profítis Ilías after the little church built at the top. It is also reported as Élympos. The village was built after the 10th century by the inhabitants of ancient Vrykoúnta, whose ruins lie some 10 km to the north, and ancient Nísyros of Saría, the two of them being among the four powerful towns of the ancient Karpathian tetrápolis. The people of Vrykoúnta, tired and decimated by the continuous piratical raids, at first settled in an area to the east of Avlóna called Exepitaréa, meaning eviction. This happened between the 8th and the 9th c. Then they settled in contemporary Olympos, which, due to its altitude (250 m) and the steepness of the ground to the west, was ideal for safe settlement in the dark and insecure years of the Middle Ages. In those days, the houses facing the west coasts of Kárpathos remained unpainted so that they could not be discerned from the sea. The village was surrounded by fortifications. That plain and austere Dorian tradition and social structure of the inhabitants has to a great extent been preserved to date. The first social classes were the despiéres, who were farmers and lived inside the fortified settlement, and the tsombánides, who were stock-breeders and lived outside the fortification. In the years of the Turkish occupation, the kanakárides (singular: kanakáris; see Morals and Customs), who owned the largest plots of land in Avlóna, the breadbasket of Olympos, emer-

The renowned Olympos!

THE SETTLEMENTS

The west side of Olympos to the Karpathian Sea

THE SETTLEMENTS

Old woman of Olympos wearing a traditional costume at a souvenir shop

ged as the new social class. The lack of roads and the difficulty in communication with the other villages of the central and south Kárpathos isolated Olympos and, as a result, the mountain village maintained the morals, customs and traditions of its distant past. The women still wear their traditional costumes every day and the houses are internally arranged as they were in the past, with the kélos and the sofádes. The heavy transport tasks inside the village are carried out by donkeys (the streets are too narrow for cars) and the people use many Dorian suffixes and words forgotten by the modern Greek language. Rural works are fulfilled in the traditional way —even two of the windmills adorning the saddle of Profítis Ilías are still used for milling wheat. The entire setting around Olympos, together with the village itself, is unique and captivating! Wild and steep mountain slopes, cliffs and gorges surround the village and, quite often, when fog is formed, an absolutely otherworldly atmosphere is created! The houses are amphitheatrically built on the slope of Mount Profítis Ilías and have cubic shape. They are yellow, indigo, white and ochre, while the village is a typical example of medieval settlement: narrow and intricate alleys connected by steps. Cars reach as far as the parking area at the entrance of the village (after you have stopped to take some pictures from afar). Walk up the main cobbled pavement alongside small shops selling tourist items, cafes and restaurants, before you get to the central square of the village called platý, which is dominated by the 16th c. church of Koímisi tis Theotókou (the Dormition). This quarter is called mésa kástro (inner castle) and is clear proof of the former fortification. On the saddle of the mountain, but in other places as well, you can see the U-shaped windmills, the distinctive feature of Olympos. It is only natural that there is a museum in Olympos: the beautiful and rich folklore museum of Hatzivassílis. You can find several traditional places to stay and you can get to Olympos either by car, as the road has been completed, or by sea from the port of Diafáni and then by shuttle bus. The municipal district of Olympos is the largest of all and comprises the entire north Kárpathos (including Saría) to the north of the village of Spóa. Other remarkable locations worth visiting are Vroukoúnta with the ruins of the ancient town and the church of Agios Ioánnis inside the cave (accessible only after hiking for 10 km from Avlóna or by sea), the cove of Trístomo (after hiking for a long time or by sea), the exceptional beach of Agios Minás and, of course, the islet of Saría. The population of the village is approximately 350 people and the distance from Pigádia is 48 km.

Pigádia

The capital of Kárpathos! The heart of the island is here; the municipal and provincial authorities as well as all state authorities are based in the village: police, port authorities, customs, post office, health centre and the main port of the island. The population is almost 3,000 people. The name means "wells" in Greek and this is so due to water bores that must have existed in the area. It is built on the site of ancient Potídaion or Poseídion, the most important and powerful town of the ancient Karpathian tetrápolis. On the coasts of the bay of Vrónti or Pigádia, where the capital is situated, there are traces of continuous habitation since the Minoan period (1500 BC). The acropolis of the ancient town was built in the Mycenaean period (1200

The church of Koímisi tis Theotókou at "Platý" of Olympos

THE SETTLEMENTS

The footwalk above the coast is full of cafes and souvenir shops

BC) at the top of the cliff Kávos that towers over the port. However, Pigádia is a relatively recent town because it developed immediately after the capital was transferred from Apéri, in the early 20th c. The town is to the SE of the island and is amphitheatrically built along the coast. Although there are not many traditional architectural elements, as it happens in other villages of the island, it is a beautiful and modern coastal little town. The bay forms two deepest points at the edges of the town, while, in combination with the skerries and the massive bulk of Mount Traoúnia to the north, a perfect natural port is formed. The coastal road and the footwalk running alongside and above the road are the heart of the town, especially in summer months, when the town is full of visitors. Cafes, restaurants, taverns, bars and souvenir shops create a cosmopolitan atmosphere and a walk by the sea is always enjoyable. The next parallel road is the commercial axis of the town. Pigádia and the wider area offer a great number of hotels as well as other accommodation facilities. Admire the beauty of the provincial building, which also accommodates the state museum, and its square, in Italian colonial architectural style, the open-air Poseidónio amphitheatre, and the church of Evangelístria. The impressive mo-

View of Pigádia from "Kávos" above the port

A journey in the Aegean sea

The Italian provincial building at Pigádia

nument you can see below the Town Hall, at the level of the marina, is dedicated to the Greek flight lieutenant Konstantinos Iliákis, who was killed while trying to intercept a Turkish fighter over Kárpathos in 2006. Within a very short distance, in the area of Áfoti, near the big hotels and right on the coast, you can see the ruins of the Early Christian basilica of Agia Foteiní with the marble columns. Further below, at Vrónti, the beautiful beaches of Pigádia open up within a radius of two kilometres. Enjoy crystal clear waters, golden sand and pebbles. The two wonderful churches of Panagía Larniótissa and Agia Kyriakí, along the road to Ardáni, after the rock of Kávos and above the port, belong to the wider area of Pigádia.

Monument dedicated to Flight Lieutenant Iliákis

FOTO: Boštjan Henigman

The cosmopolitan town of Pigádia

THE SETTLEMENTS

View of the town from the nearby beach
(photo: Ilías Makrís)

Do not miss them! Pigádia is within 16 km from the airport.

Pylés

Pylés is a very pretty little village on the west slopes of Mount Lástos, the last of the four mountain villages of central Kárpathos. There are several versions with regard to the derivation of the name (meaning gates in Greek) but the most possible is associated with the gates the settlement used to have at its entrance. It was built in the 17th c. at an altitude of 300 m and faces the Karpathian and the Libyan seas. The views of neighbouring Kásos and the mountains of Crete are breathtaking, especially in the sunset. Many of the 250 inhabitants of the village are descended from the tortured Kásos as their ancestors escaped their island after the holocaust of 1824 during the Greek War of Independence. The houses have blue windows and are lost amid bougainvilleas and flowers. There are two churches, Panagía (the Virgin) and Stavrós (Holy Cross), a tavern and a cafe. The locals should be praised for their efforts to create an agricultural museum, which includes even living domestic animals. You should visit it. It is at the entrance of the settlement, close to the parking area and above the war monument. The beach of 'Adeia and the verdant gorge of Flaskiá belong to Pylés. The village lies within 14 km from Pigádia.

The yards at Pylés are full of flowers

Pylés: the sun is shining in the background

The agricultural museum at Pylés

Spóa

This is the last village before the boundaries of the municipal district of Olympos. The first thing the visitor sees is the towering windmills at the junction of the roads from Pigádia and Mesochóri. In one of these mills you can find refreshments. The village is amphitheatrically built at the narrowest point of the island –the distance from the east to the west coast is only 6 km–, on a hill looking like an ancient acropolis as well as on the terraces of nearby elevations. In the central square you can find cafes and taverns. The locals love their village very much and they are famous for their hospitality and the

The little port of Agios Nikólaos at Spóa

Golden clouds above Spóa
(photo: Karpathiakí newspaper)

Foiníki

Foiníki is the pretty little port of Arkása, only 3 km to the north, which until a few years ago served the communication of Kárpathos with the adjacent island of Kásos. Until several decades ago, larger ships from Crete and Piraeus used to arrive in Foiníki. The landmark of the little port is the country church of Agios Nikólaos at the top of the hill above the village. In local taverns you can find fresh and a lot of fish brought by the fishing boats that dock at the port. There are sufficient accommodation facilities. At the beach you can see the monument erected in honour of the seven brave young men who, after the revolt of 1944, left the port aboard the boat Imakoláta and sailed to Alexandria of Egypt in order to bring the marvelous news of liberation to the exiled Greek government. Foiníki has a population of 30 people and the distance to Pigádia is 8 km.

sardines they catch with their fishing boats, which dock at the little port of the village, Agios Nikólaos, 6 km below Spóa. This is a picturesque and quiet fishing village with accommodation facilities and taverns. Within a short distance from Agios Nikólaos, you can see the ruins of the 5th c. Early Christian basilica of Eftambatoúsa. Spóa has a population of about 300 people and the distance to Pigádia is 26 km.

The wonderful Foiníki

SIGHTS

Despite its small size, Kárpathos has lots of sights you should visit. Castles, museums, Early Christian basilicas as well as more recent monuments, places of interest and areas of particular natural beauty are scattered all over the island. Below you can find the most important details of these sights so that you can make your arrangements.

Castles

Paliókastro, ARKASA: at the top of the peninsula, next to the village, ruins of Cyclopean fortifications from the Mycenaean and subsequent periods.

Paliókastro, *Koráki*, VOLADA: clearly visible Byzantine and Frank fortifications on the hill between the villages of Apéri and Voláda. It is also

The Sókastro at Lefkós

reported in the paragraph of Voláda because access is easier from that village although it is known as the castle of Apéri.

Sókastro, LEFKOS: on the islet off the coast of the holiday settlement, ruins of a 9th c. Byzantine fortification.

Vroukoúnta, OLYMPOS: on the hill of Pyrgálli, surviving ruins of the fortification of ancient Vroukoúnta.

Acropolis of ancient Potídaion, PIGADIA: fortification ruins at the top of the cliff towering above the port. Traces that have been found date the acropolis back to the Mycenaean period (1200 BC).

Acropolis of Sáros, SARIA: on the west slope of the hill of Kastéllo, ruins of fortifications, possibly of ancient Nísyros.

Early Christian Basilicas

Agia Anastasia, ARKASA: at the foot of Paliókastro, 5th c. AD amazing mosaics!

Unnamed, LEFKOS: an arch of an Early Christian basilica has been found in the sea

Vasilikés of Vroukoúnta, OLYMPOS: ruins of three basilicas have been found at ancient Vroukoúnta

Agios Theódoros, OLYMPOS: ruins of three basilicas have been found at Trístomo

Agia Foteiní, PIGADIA: 5th c. AD marble columns at the beach of Áfoti!

Unnamed, PIGADIA: a three-aisled basilica with narthex at Kefáli

Agia Sofia, SARIA: beautiful mosaic and fallen columns in the cove of Palátia

Unnamed, SARIA: three-aisled basilica with narthex on the hill of Kastéllo

Eftambatoúsa, SPOA: 5th c. AD basilica near the little port of Agios Nikólaos.

The mosaic in the basilica of Arkása

The archaeological museum at Pigádia

Museums

Archaeological Museum of Kárpathos, PIGADIA. Next to the provincial building. The first room of the museum includes finds from the Neolithic period, the Minoan rural house and the Mycenaean settlement as well as finds from the necropolis. The second room is dedicated to historic times and the visitor can admire finds from the Hellenistic and the Roman periods. The third room includes finds from the Early Christian and Byzantine periods. The museum is open in the summer at an admission charge. Tel.: 2245023441.

Folklore, OTHOS. On the central street of the village. Reconstruction of a house and the daily life of the locals. Tel.: 2245031460

Folklore, MENETES. Next to the holy rock, accommodated in an old little church. Exhibits include implements and tools intended for household and rural works, objects of traditional art, musical instruments as well as a collection of photographs taken by locals. Tel.: 2245081190

Folklore, archaeological, ARKASA. Behind the main street of the village, in a large room with a magnificent pebbled floor. Folklore exhibits and ecclesiastical objects from the Early Christian basilica of Agia Anastasia. Amazing dolphin skeletons found on the coast of Arkása. Tel.: 2245061284

Folklore, OLYMPOS. A private initiative of the local artist V. Hatzivassilis. Below Platý, it accommodates the works of the artist but also provides a picture of the traditional life of the locals and a wealth of folklore information.

The folklore museum of Menetés is accommodated in an old church

KARPATHOS | 71

Museum of Arkása

Exhibits from the small museum of Pylés

Folklore, rural life, PYLES. Above the parking area at the entrance of the village. A beautiful museum with folklore exhibits and a reconstruction of the rural life of the locals as it includes a little plot of land and living domestic animals (donkeys, hens, goats and the indispensable sheepdog!) stabled in the museum.

Ecclesiastical, OLYMPOS. Accommodated in an auxiliary space of the church of Koímisi tis Theotókou, it includes ecclesiastical heirlooms from north Kárpathos.

Churches

Agia Aikaterini, SARIA CANAL. At the narrowest point of the canal, on the site of the ancient temple of Porthmeíos Poseidon.

Agia Kyriakí, PIGADIA. After Larniótissa, a white little church offering a wonderful view and lots of facilities donated by the faithful.

Agia Sofia, SARIA. At Palátia, a pretty 9th c. little church built on the site of an Early Christian basilica with mosaics; columns and ruins of an ancient temple all around.

Agioi Apóstoloi, AMMOOPI. A beautiful country church at the top of the peninsula, above the sea.

Agia Kyriakí (Pigádia)

A journey in the Aegean sea

Agia Sofia (Saría)

Agios Mámmas (Menetés)

Agios Georgios Vassón, APERI. Inactive restored monastery with a long historical background, founded circa 17th c.

Agios Georgios, LEFKOS. At Áno Lefkós, a 13th c. Byzantine little church.

Agios Ioánnis (Ablation of John the Baptist's head), VRYKOUNTA. Inside a carved rock near the coast of ancient Vroukoúnta.

Agios Mámmas, MENETES. Conical little church with 14th c. wall paintings at Exíles.

Agios Minás, AGIOS MINAS. At the

Taxiárchis Monastery (Mt. Lástos)

The cathedral of Karpathos

top of the hill, next to the namesake beach, a snow-white little church with a wonderful view.

Agios Panteleímon, STES. A beautiful church in an idyllic setting.

Archistrátigos Michael-Taxiárchis, LASTOS. Inactive monastery with lots of auxiliary facilities.

Eisódia tis Theotókou, APERI. The cathedral of Kárpathos and Kásos.

Evangelístria, PIGADIA. On the first parallel to the coastal street. The cathedral of the capital, with several aisles and a dome.

Koímisi tis Theotókou, MENETES. On the holy rock, a 19th c. church with an amazing bell-tower. Two marble columns from the basilica of Agia Anastasia of Arkása. Very impressive church on a wonderful paved square, with several aisles and auxiliary spaces.

Koímisi tis Theotókou, OTHOS. A small 17th c. church.

Koímisi tis Theotókou, OLYMPOS. On the central square of the village, remarkable iconostasis and 16th c. wall paintings.

Kyrá Panagiá, KYRA PANAGIA. One of the island's symbols. A small church on the cliff above the famous beach that adorns postcards from Kárpathos.

Agios Loukas, APELLA. A 12th c. church carved into the rock before the beach.

The church of Panagía at Menetés

Agios Minás

The stunning iconostasis of Panagía in Olympos

Panagía Larniótissa (Pigádia)

Panagiá Vrysianí (the Virgin's Birthday), MESOCHORI. Flowing water considered holy. One of the greatest celebrations takes place here.

Panagía Larniótissa, PIGADIA. The annual religious meeting of the people of Pigádia takes place in a verdant area that includes facilities for the great celebration of September 7.

Panagiá Plagiá (the Virgin's Birthday), VOLADA. The pretty 18th c. main church of the village.

Panagia, MERTONAS. At the springs

Ypapantí (Arkása)

Agios Loukás (Ápella)

SIGHTS

Kyrá Panagiá

A journey in the Aegean sea

of Mértonas, before Kyrá Panagiá, 12th c. wall paintings.

Hypapantí, ARKASA. The main church of Arkása with the tall belltower. Several aisles.

Locations of Particular Natural Beauty and Interest

Lástos Plateau. Follow the uphill road to the right after the village of Voláda and, within a few kilometres and, after you have been fascinated by the breath-taking view of the Libyan and the Karpathian seas, thanks to the altitude, you get to the plateau of Lástos. It is a wild landscape with low vegetation. The road that crosses it ends at a pretty little tavern at an altitude of 900 m. After a while you can find the hiking route to the top of Lástos, at 1215 m, while soon to the left you can find the start of the hiking route to the gorge of Flaskiá. On the plateau there are several scattered country churches and inactive monasteries, most important of them being Taxiárchis Archistrátigos (Archangel Commander-in-Chief) and the church of Agia Marina with the large cross.

Flaskiá Gorge. A hiking route that starts from the plateau of Lástos and ends at 'Adeia Beach of the village of Pylés after crossing the verdant Flaskiá Gorge, which is full of flowing waters.

Limniótis Gorge. Halfway between Apéri and Aháta Beach. Research has been conducted but the gorge has not been exploited so as to become fully accessible and be provided with suitable facilities. However, there are stunning colourful stalagmites and stalactites although the entrance to the cave is rather low (the visitor should lower the head in

"Kalí Límni", the highest peak in Karpathos

The starting point of the descent to Flaskiá Gorge

order to enter). The rich internal geological decorations require that you have a torch in order to admire them!

Saría Island. The island of pirates! It is separated from north Kárpathos by a narrow 200 m wide canal and it is assumed that in antiquity it was the site where ancient Nísyros was built. A few people lived in the area of 'Argos until the 1970s before they left for Olympos. Today it is a primary destination of cruisers and boats sailing from Pigádia and mainly from Diafáni. Because there are no docking facilities, the boats tie up at the rocks of Palátia, where you can find a pretty pebbled beach. In the elevations around Palátia you can see and visit some buildings of peculiar vaulted shapes. They were used by Saracen pirates in the Middle Ages, who had turned the small island into one of the greatest hideaways of Mediterranean corsairs. At Palátia you can also see the 9th c. church of Agia Sofia, built on the site of a previous mosaic floor of a 5th c. Early Christian basilica, while all around you can see scattered parts of ancient columns possibly belonging to a sanctuary, before they were used in the basilica. The little church of Profítis Zacharías stands at the top of the imposing mountain that rises on the other side, while a little further you can find the ruins of the previously mentioned settlement of 'Argos. Another renowned and exotic beach of Saría is Alimoúnta, a little to the north of the cove of Palátia. The island is crossed by a splendid hiking route from the narrowest point of the canal as far as Palátia. There is no Wi-Fi connection or any other provision here and the sense that you are on a desert island at the edge of the Aegean, with your only company being wild goats and seabirds, will calm and reward you! If you are lucky enough, you may see some Mediterranean monk seals monachus-monachus lying in the sun or diving into the emerald waters of Saría.

KARPATHOS

Palátia of Saría offers dock to cruisers

Trístomo. It means three entrances or mouths. Well, this is actually true since the two rocks at the entrance of the bay form three entrances to this amazing natural port. Access is only on foot from Avlóna of Olympos or by sea, after docking at the small jetty in front of the church of Panormítis Taxiárchis. There are no inhabitants although you can see some buildings on the coasts. Until the 19th c. it was widely used by pirates and the revolted Greek fleet of 1821 due to the natural protection and shelter it offered.

Typical building of the Saracen settlement in Saría

The impressive closed cove at Trístomo

Other Sights

The Wreck. In the military area of Cape Lígki there are some remains of an Italian wrecked ship -only the bow- which is visible and highly photographed from all the coasts of Afiártis to the east.

The Mills. The typical windmills of the Aegean Islands can also be seen in the north part of Kárpathos, shortly before the village of Spóa and along the saddle of the mountain of Olympos. They belong to the category of *ksetrocháris* (both their roof as well as the sails could be moved so that the mill could operate under all wind directions), but mainly to the category of *petalóschimos* (U-shaped). They were widely used in the Greek archipelago in the period of the Frank occupation (13th and 14th c.) and earlier. Two of them are still in use in Olympos!

Typical U-shaped windmill in Olympos

SUGGESTED TRIPS

Due to the large number of settlements and places of interest, it is rather difficult for the visitors to explore Kárpathos extensively unless they have made a specific plan in advance as the days are never enough. In this chapter, we would like to suggest some trips on condition that you stay on the island up to one week and you have your own means of transport. Our starting point will be the capital of Pigádia. All suggested routes are 99% on asphalt roads. Hiking routes are presented in the next chapter. Get one of the road maps of ROAD or ORAMA Editions, your camera, and press throttle!

Olympos: an eerie landscape...
(photo: Níkos Filippákis, taken from Afrodíti Hotel)

SUGGESTED TRIPS

A journey in the Aegean sea

SUGGESTED TRIPS

KARPATHOS | 91

South Kárpathos

Start from Pigádia, take the road to the airport and drive slightly uphill as you leave the capital behind you. When you see the first sign indicating Ardáni, turn left and follow the road down to the sea. The first large beach you find is called Poulioú Potámi. Continue and turn right at the beach, to the south, and after a while you start seeing the lacy coastline of Ammoopí. The first beach you see is Mikrí (small) Ammoopí and then comes Megáli (large) Ammoopí or Péra 'Ammos, which is more cosmopolitan. The little church of Agioi Apóstoloi separates the peninsula from Votsalákia, another small beach with equally blue waters. Now the road runs uphill in the direction of Lakkí, which can be considered the centre of the settlement. You get to a junction and turn left. The road leads to Kastélia, an area with plenty of accommodation facilities. At the end of the road you get to a rocky but organized beach. If you continue a little beyond this junction, there is another junction. Turn left and you reach Fókia Beach, less cosmopolitan but very pretty as well. You see, Ammoopí is full of little coves that

The view of Pigádia as you are leaving the airport is wonderful

Megáli Ammoopí with the little church of Agioi Apóstoloi to the far left

form different successive beaches. Carry on uphill and get to the main road Pigádia-Airport, where you turn left. After 5 km and after crossing a landscape of wild beauty and deep gorges, you drive down the mountain of Kefálas and start entering the plain of **Afiártis**! The flat area opens up before you as far as the airport and the elevation of Cape Kastéllo, the southernmost point of the island. As soon as you enter the plain, you start seeing junctions to the left that lead to the beaches of Damátria, Christoú Pigádi (very nice indeed), and Prassonísi. The area to the right is called Kípos tou Afiárti (garden of Afiártis) because it is full of vegetable gardens belonging to the inhabitants of Menetés. Continue straight and you are bound to see lots of surfers enjoying their favourite sport to the left. These are the beaches of Vathá, Limní and Makrýs Gialós, all ideal for surf lovers and wannabe sailors. You have now reached the airport and the military area. Far to the left, at the edge of the military camp, you can see the bow of an Italian old wreck rising among the cliffs. At the airport you have to turn right and at the next junction turn again left as if you wanted to move around the airport. As soon as the enclosure ends, you have the south beaches and the Libyan Sea to your left. The beach with the kite surfs is called Agrilopótamos and is ideal for this water sport. Kárpathos caters for all tastes! You may find some sectors of dirt road but do not worry, it is only for a while. Continue straight

KARPATHOS

The square at Arkása

ahead to the west and you get to the southwest cape of Agios Theódoros. Below the namesake little church there is a rock-cut pretty beach. Turn right to the north and follow the road to **Arkása**, while to the left you can see the island of Kásos. After 5 km, you get to the largest village of the west side of the island. The first junction to the left takes you to the beach of Agios Nikólaos, the most known beach of Arkása. Return to

Monument dedicated to the heroic trip of liberation at Foiníki

On the road from Menetés to Pigádia

the main road and, before entering the village, turn again left to the Early Christian basilica of Agia Anastasia. Admire the exquisite mosaic and the scattered building elements as well as the little church of Agia Sofia with the baptistery. The mountain bulk emerging in front of you is Paliókastro, the acropolis of ancient Arkeseía. You can only access it on foot. Continue again along the road to the village after driving over the little bridge. Park at the entrance of the village and take a walk. The museum of Arkása is to the right of the main footwalk and includes interesting exhibits and a wonderful pebbled floor. The main square of the village is at the end of the footwalk. Within only 2 km from Arkása, you can visit **Foiníki**, a picturesque little port with lots of taverns serving fresh fish. Return to Arkása and follow the signs to Pigádia. At the next junction, turn left. After approximately one kilometre, there is a sign to the left pointing to a dirt road, which, after 500 m, will take you to the church of Agios Mámmas with the impressive shape. Follow again the main road and, after 3 km, you reach the stunning village of **Menetés**. The view of the village is amazing! Visit the church of Panagía (the Virgin) on the holy rock and the adjacent small folklore museum. On exiting the village, you can see a monument dedicated to the revolt of 1944. This is yet another site recommended for taking good photographs of the village although the best point is the hill opposite the holy rock. Continue and get to the main road Pigádia-Airport, where you turn left. After 5 km you will enter the capital. The tour of south Kárpathos covers an overall distance of about 60 km.

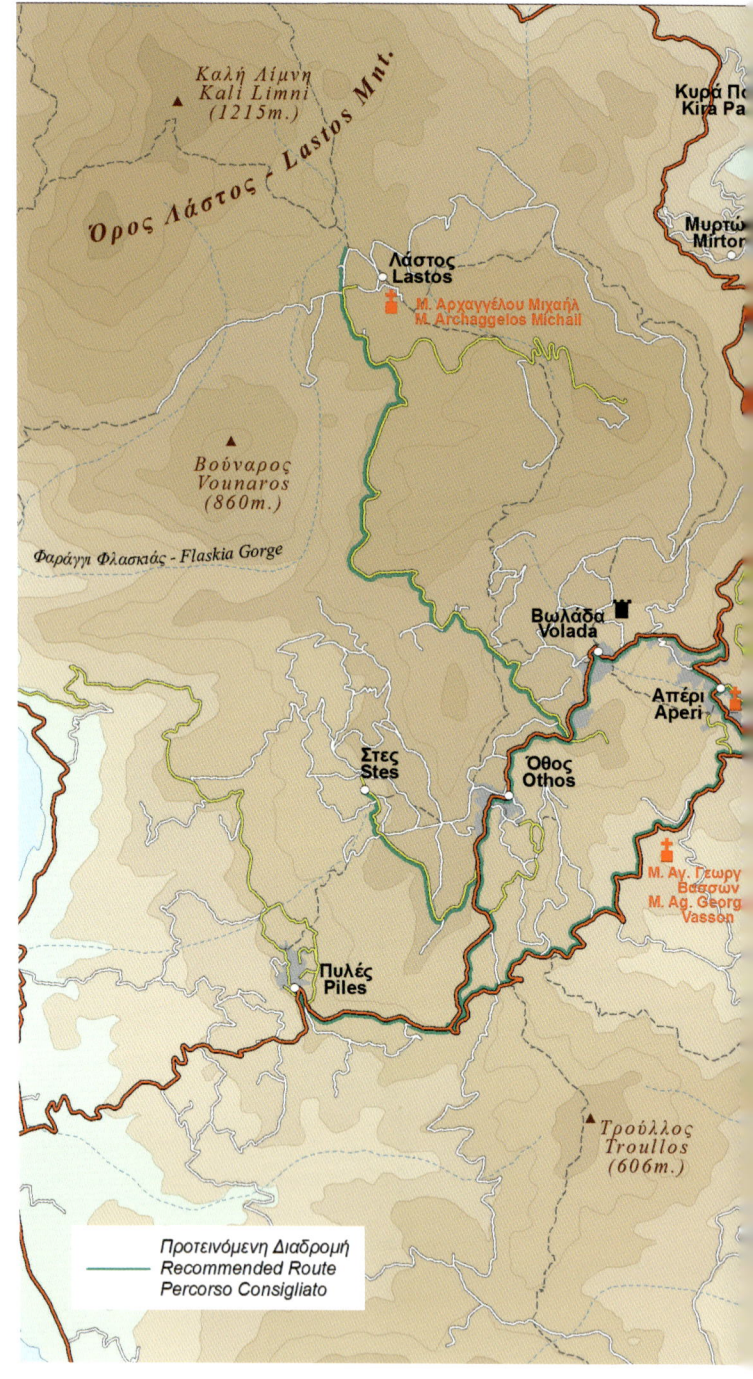

Villages of Central Kárpathos

Take the road leading to Apéri and Olympos. Leave the town behind and drive alongside the coast of Pigádia. The beaches of Áfoti, with the Early Christian basilica of Agia Foteiní, and Vrónti are to your right. After 2 km (in the area of DEI –Public Power Corporation) the road turns left and runs uphill in the pine forest. Three kilometres after the junction turn left in order to cross the village of **Apéri**, the former capital of Kárpathos with the mansions. Here, after a little bridge to your left, is the seat of the bishop of Kárpathos. Continue uphill along the narrow road and from the bend, after exiting Apéri, you can see the pretty village of **Voláda**. If you want, you can stop and, from the centre of the village, walk up the hill of Koráki, where you can see the fortification of the medieval castle. At the exit of the village turn right following the sign indicating **Lástos**. The road runs uphill but is really wonderful. At first it crosses a verdant area and then enters the wild beauty of the plateau of Mount Lástos, the highest mountain of Kárpathos. Before reaching the plateau, admire the unique views of Kásos and Crete to the left! Cross the plateau and get to the end of the road, at the beginning of the path le-

The pretty little church of Anástasi (the Resurrection) at Vrónti

The village of Apéri

ading to the peak of Kalí Límni (1215 m). You are now 900 m high and the only sign of life is a pretty little tavern. Return to Voláda and when you reach the margins of the village, turn right and, after 2 km, you get to **Óthos**! It is the highest of the villages of central Kárpathos (510 m). You

View of Voláda from the hill with the huge Cross

The village of Óthos

KARPATHOS | 99

Traditional cafe at Pylés

The gate to the monastery Agios Geórgios Vassón

can visit the folklore museum and taste the delicious sausages produced in the village. Five hundred metres after Óthos turn right and, after one kilometre of scenic drive, you get to the idyllic **Stes**, a location full of trees and vegetable gardens exploited by Óthos. Go back and now turn right to the west. After 3 km you reach **Pylés**, the last of the villages of central Kárpathos. Right at the entrance of the village, in the area of the parking space, you should visit the remarkable agricultural museum with the domestic animals! Pylés is a small but beautiful village with exceptional views of the west coasts and Kásos. Take the road back and exactly after one and a half kilometres turn slightly right at the junction. There is no reason to see all the villages again. This route is also beautiful and passes from the **monastery of Agios Geórgios Vassón,** the only monastery of the island, even though it is inactive. After approximately 5 km, you get to the entrance of the village of Apéri. From that point onward, you can follow the signs and, after a wonderful drive of 5 km, you reach the pretty beach of **Aháta**. Along the road you can see the stunning cave of Limniótis. Go back, turn left and return to Pigádia through the same road. The tour of the villages of central Kárpathos covers an overall distance of approximately 55 km.

The beautiful beach at Aháta

SUGGESTED TRIPS

102 | A journey in the Aegean sea

Lefkós, Mesochóri, Spóa, East Coasts

Take again the coastal road to the villages and Olympos. At the junction to Apéri, turn left towards the entrance of the village but immediately turn again left in order to follow the sign indicating *Agios Geórgios Vassón Monastery*. Drive past the monastery and at the next junction continue straight to the west. Bypass the village of Pylés and now, as you drive downward, you can enjoy the splendid view of the Karpathian Sea in front of you! At the junction before the sea, turn right to the north. The road is full of bends but the landscape is picturesque and rewarding. About 5 km after you have turned, the setting becomes wilder and prettier. The forest with the pinus brutia pines floods the steep slopes of Lástos down to the sea. Exactly 5.4 km after you have turned north, you get to the end of Flaskiá Gorge, while a road to the left leads to the beach of **Ádeia**. Continue straight along the main road, which now runs uphill but offers an amazing view of the sea to the left. Within 7 km after the junction to Ádeia, you get to the junction of Áno Lefkós and the nearby pretty little Byzantine church of Agios Geórgios. Turn left into the descending road that leads to the resort of **Káto Lefkós**, where you reach after about driving for 4 km in a pine forest. The successive beaches formed by the scenic bays will remind you of Ammoopí. To the left of the coast as you reach the sea, you can see the beaches of Potáli, Gialoú Horáfi, Mikró Limanáki and Frangolimniónas. The island with the ruins of the Byzantine castle off the coast is called Sókastro. In the area of Lefkós, before the beach, there is a tank surviving from the Roman years. Take the same road to return to 'Ano Lefkos, where you turn left, and after 4 km, at the sign indicating **Mesochóri**, turn again left. When you reach the short tunnel, stop and take some photos of the stunning landscape, with the village hanging above the cliff and the mountains of Olympos in the background emerging from the endless blue horizon! Park at the entrance of the village. A walk around the scenic Mesochóri is a good

As you walk down Mt. Lástos the view of Kásos and the Libyan Sea is amazing

The Sókastro dominates the sea of Lefkós

idea. Visit the pride of the locals, the church of Panagiá Vrysianí with the cool holy waters. The walk ends at Skópi Square, at the edge of the cliff! Return to the junction before the village and turn left. After 4 km you get to the main junction of the two coastal roads of the island with the road that leads to the north. This is where the old windmills of **Spóa** stand, with the village being one kilometre further ahead. In one of the windmills you can find a canteen. The windmills were built on this site on purpose because this is the meeting point of the west and east winds that blow

The windmills before Spóa

The little church of Panagía at the verdant Mertóni

from the respective sides of the island through the gorges and reach this narrowest point of their routes. Spóa is to your right. You can drive down and find a place to park if you want to wander around the village. The road continues downhill and, after 6 km, you reach the picturesque **Agios Nikólaos**, the little port of Spóa, where you can also see the ruins of the Early Christian basilica of Eftambatoúsa. Do not fail to taste fresh fish! Drive back to Spóa and turn left at the junction with the main road Spóa-Olympos. At the main junction of the windmills, turn again left to the south. Although the road is narrow, the magnificent landscape will definitely fascinate you! The steep cliffs and the deep gorges that open up to the endless blue of the sea to the left are a sight the visitor rarely sees! After 5 km you get to a junction whose left branch leads to the beach of **Ápella**, a beach of exquisite beauty and one of the most

The magical beach at Ápella

The famous beach of Kyrá Panagiá

famous of Kárpathos. Along the road and before the beach you can also admire the rock-cut 12th c. little church of Agios Loukás. Drive uphill and turn left into the main road. After 7 km of a winding section of the road and after crossing the verdant area of Mertónas, turn left at the sign indicating to the beach of **Kyrá Panagiá**. Drive down 3 km through pines and go past the location of Katódio with the springs of fresh water. You have now reached the famous beach with the namesake red-domed little church on the rock to the right. As you can see, it is a particularly cosmopolitan beach as there are taverns, cafes, shops and plenty of accommodation facilities. Go back to the main road and, at the junction you find after 1 km, turn left into the ring road of Apéri, which takes you to the end of the village. Drive for the remaining 7 km to Pigádia, where you started from. The overall distance of this route is about 80 km.

View of Pigádia from the junction to Apéri

KARPATHOS | 107

SUGGESTED TRIPS

A journey in the Aegean sea

SUGGESTED TRIPS

KARPATHOS

North Karpathos starts after the church of Taxiárches at Spóa

North Kárpathos

Start from Pigádia and drive along the coastal road to the villages and Olympos. When you get to the junction leading to Apéri, follow the signs pointing to Spóa-Olympos and drive along the ring road to the right. Drive once again the difficult but fascinating 16 km to Spóa. Go past the amazing private church of Taxiárches (Archangels) after the village and enter the administrative boundaries of Olympos. Things are different now as the landscape becomes darker and wilder. The road has been completed in recent years and is still in good condition. There are no remarkable spots or settlements along the overall distance of 22 km from Spóa to the capital of north Kárpathos. In the last 2 km you will be amazed by the view of the dreamy village. This is **Olympos**, the village where time has stopped! There are several points along the winding road that are ideal for taking photos. Vehicles are prohibited inside the village and you should park at the entrance. Walk along the narrow alleys and see the smiling women of Olympos wearing their traditional costumes. It is only certain that you will be carried away to another time... Visit Platý Square with the church of Panagiá, the striking windmills on the saddle of Mount Profítis Ilías, the folklore museum of Hatzivassilis, and try to "assimilate" the superb beauty of the landscape because there is nothing like that – at least in Greece. Leave Olympos and turn left at the junction leading to the village. After 2 km the magnificent picture of Olympos still dominates the setting. A sharp left turn (indicated by a sign) takes you to **Avlóna**, the rural settlement of Olympos, after 3 km. It is situated on the namesake plateau and, as you drive

Olympos

SUGGESTED TRIPS

View of Olympos from a country church near Avlóna

The scenic Diafáni

down the road, the view is impressive. Return to the main road and turn left. The road runs downhill with continuous bends and, after 4 km, you get to **Diafáni**, the beautiful port of Olympos. It is the second port of the island, built alongside a pretty pebbled beach. There are several hotels and rooms to rent as well as lots of taverns and cafes. The port is the starting point for a trip to the nearby island of Saría, the amazing Trístomo and Vroukoúnta. Now take the road back to Olympos. After the village and about halfway to Spóa there is a dirt road to the left that, after 5 km,

Olives at the beach of Agios Minás (view from the road)

KARPATHOS | 113

takes you to the pretty black beach of Agios Minás with the namesake snow-white little church towering on the hill to the left. Increased attention is required because the road is steep. Return to Pigádia via the same road you drove to come to Olympos. You only have to set off early because you need quite a lot of time for the 50 km back. The tour of north Kárpathos covers an overall distance of about 115 km.

Saría, Trístomo, Vroukoúnta

In order to complete your exploration and have a full picture of Kárpathos, you should not fail to visit these three magnificent areas in the northernmost part of the island. Access to Saría is only by sea, as it happens with the two other locations of **Trístomo** and **Vroukoúnta**, although they are also accessed via hiking routes and paths starting from Avlóna. This information is included in the special chapter dedicated to the hiking routes of the island.

The north part of Karpathos with Trístomo and Saría
(photo: Giórgos Kanákis)

ALTERNATIVE TOURISM

The mountains, the coasts and the sea of Kárpathos provide the ideal conditions for all kinds of alternative tourism, which has greatly been developed in recent years. There are enterprises activating in any kind of alternative tourism and providing the facilities, the equipment and the know-how to the lovers of every specific activity.

Hiking Routes

Hiking along ancient natural routes has lately become very popular in Greece; Kárpathos is one of the top destinations among Greek islands. The relief of the ground and variations in the landscape are very helpful but if it had not been for hiking lovers, nothing would have happened. The extremely active local *Club of Mountain and Sea Friends of Kárpathos* has played an important role and has opened, cleared and signed the 30 delightful hiking routes. The only requirement is the possession of **No. 201 Kárpathos - Kásos hiking map of ROAD Nakas Cartography**, which can be found in a great number of local shops and will tremendously help you with your explorations. The network of hiking routes on the island covers an overall distance of 200 km. Here are the main routes in every part of the island (beauty of route rated 1-5 the best).

SOUTH KARPATHOS

The south and central parts of the island include 18 signed routes:

Route 1
Pigádia ❶ – Agia Kyriakí Church ❷ – Panagía Larniótissa ❸

Type: Circular - Length: 4 km - Non-stop time: 1 h 45' - Altitude Differences: ±250 m, Beauty: 2.

A short beautiful route on the mountainous peninsula to the south of the capital with a wonderful view and the two splendid little country churches of Pigádia.

Route 2
Menetés ❹ – Pigádia ❶

Type: Crossing - Length: 6.2 km - Non-stop time: 2 h 45' - Altitude Differences: +30 m - 350 m - Beauty: 2.

An interesting route connecting Pigádia with the village of Menetés through a small plain to the east of Pigádia.

Route 3
Óthos ❺ – Agios Georgios Vassón Monastery ❻ - Pigádia ❶

Type: Crossing - Length: 10.1 km - Non-stop time: 3 h 30' - Altitude Differences: +0 m - 500 m - Beauty: 2.

A route connecting the highest village of the island, Óthos, with the capital of Pigádia. The path passes from Agios Georgios Vassón Monastery and the rock-cut tombs of the medieval period, which are called Táfos tou Digení (tomb of Digenís). It also passes close to Spiliá tou Poseidóna (Cave of Poseidon) at Mýloi, before it reaches Pigádia.

Route 4
Menetés ❹ - Arkása (Arkeseía) ❼

Type: Crossing - Length: 7.7 km - Non-stop time: 2 h 45' - Altitude Differences: +190 m - 450 m - Beauty: 3.

A very pretty path that starts from the beautiful village of Menetés and, after running close to the little church of Agios Mámmas with the amazing shape, it leads to the historic Arkása, to the southwest of the island, which offers a beautiful view of Kásos. The route ends at Paliókastro.

Route 5
Menetés ❹ - Airport ❽

Type: Crossing - Length: 8.6 km - Non-stop time: 3 h 10' - Altitude Differences: +120 m - 450 m - Beauty: 1.

A route crossing the wildly beautiful Mount Kefálas and offering a beautiful view of Pigádia and Ammoopí. It crosses the plain of Afiártis and ends at the beach of Makrýs Gialós, a favourite destination of surfers!

Route 6
Χωριό Apéri ❾ - Agios Nikólaos Church ❿ - Pigádia ❶

Type: Crossing - Length: 8.9 km - Non-stop time: 3 h - Altitude Differences: +70 m - 330 m - Beauty: 3-first section & 1-second section

A splendid hiking route connecting the village of Apéri with Pigádia and offering a wonderful view of Apéri and Voláda. Walk down to a green location as far as the little church of Agios Nikólaos, which stands on the rocks to the north of the beach of Vrónti, and then continue alongside the pretty beach of Pigádia as far as the capital.

Route 6A
Apéri, Pigádia ⓫ - Profítis Ilías Aperíou Church ⓬
(return route)

Type: Return - Length: 4 km - Non-stop time: 1 h 30' - Altitude Differences: ±247 m - Beauty: 3.

An amazing and popular route because it ends at the little church of Profítis Ilías on the namesake mountain, where you can enjoy a splendid view of the bay of Aháta.

Route 7
Óthos ❺ - Menetés ❹

Type: Crossing - Length: 8 km - Non-stop time: 3 h 10' - Altitude Differences: +426 m - 466 m - Beauty: 3.

A nice route with a wonderful view because it runs along the ridge of Mount Troúlos.

Route 8
Óthos ❺ - Stes ⓭ - Pylés ⓮

Type: Crossing - Length: 3.2 km - Non-stop time: 1 h 10' - Altitude Differences: +90 m - 260 m - Beauty: 3.

A short and easy route crossing a verdant and idyllic landscape whose last section offers a beautiful view of the island of Kásos.

Route 9
Voláda ⓯ - Óthos ❺

Type: Crossing - Length: 2.8 km - Non-stop time: 1 h - Altitude Differences: +150 m - 80 m - Beauty: 2.

An easy and interesting route connecting the two neighbouring villages through a beautiful path on the margins of Lástos.

Route 10
Voláda ⓯ - Apéri ❾

Type: Crossing - Length: 1.8 km - Non-stop time: 40' - Altitude Differences: - 180 m - Beauty: 4.

A short but superb route that connects the two villages and passes from the little church of Stavrós (Holy Cross) with the gigantic cross, where the hiker can enjoy a wonderful view of the island as far as Pigádia and the nearby villages.

Route 11
Voláda ⑮ - Lástos Plateau ⑯ (via Agios Nikólaos)

Type: Crossing - Length: 7 km - Non-stop time: 2 h 25' - Altitude Differences: +280 m - 50 m - Beauty: 3.

The one of the two routes (11 & 12) leading to the plateau of Lástos below the peak of Kalí Límni and passing from the little church of Agios Nikólaos, with a view of the east coasts. The two routes can form a single circular route from Voláda and the margins of Kalí Límni.

Route 12
Lástos Plateau ⑯ - Voláda ⑮

Type: Crossing - Length: 6.2 km - Non-stop time: 2 h 20' - Altitude Differences: +180 m - 470 m - Beauty: 2.

The second route crossing the wildly beautiful plateau of Lástos, which may be used as a return after walking route 11.

Route 13
Lástos Plateau ⑯ - Flaskiá Gorge ⑰ - Ádeia Beach ⑱

Type: Crossing - Length: 6 km - Non-stop time: 2 h 20' - Altitude Differences: - 730 m - Beauty: 4.

A rather steep route with a grade of up to 20°, which starts from the plateau of Lástos, passes from the wonderful gorge of Flaskiá with the beautiful view and ends at the beach of Ádeia. For experienced mountain hikers only.

Route 14
Lástos Plateau ⑯ - Spóa Windmills ⑲ - Spóa ⑳

Type: Crossing - Length: 8.7 km - Non-stop time: 3 h 10' - Altitude Differences: +190 m - 610 m - Beauty: 4.

The route to Spóa is the northernmost route of the south part because the village of Spóa is the lowest point of the north part of the island. The route gives the hiker the opportunity to complete the picture of south Kárpathos. The path is old and traditional and several sections are covered with stones. It takes advantage of the relief of the island and crosses the north slopes of Kalí Límni, reaches the junction with the windmills and finally ends at the village of Spóa.

Route 15
Lástos Plateau ⑯ - Kalí Límni Peak (1,215 m) ㉑
Agios Geórgios Church ㉒

Type: Crossing - Length: 9 km - Non-stop time: 4 h 30' - Altitude Differences: + 465 m -1105 m - Beauty: 4

One of the most amazing routes of the island leading the hiker to the highest point of the island, at 1,215 m, at the peak of Kalí Límni, which offers a stunning view of mainly the north part of the island. From then on, the hiker may walk down to the west slopes of the island and get to the Byzantine church of Agios Geórgios, at Áno Lefkós. One of the most difficult routes, together with the route of Flaskiá, and a very popular one among hikers.

Route 16
Lefkós Settlement ❷❸ Mesochóri ❷❹

Type: Crossing - Length: 7.4 km - Non-stop time: 3 h - Altitude Differences: +280 - 140 m - Beauty: 3.

A traditional stone path connecting Mesochóri with the settlement of Lefkós. It runs along the northwest coast of the island, which is full of pines, and is recommended for all kinds of hikers.

Route 17
Apéri ❾ - Aháta Beach ❷❺

Type: Crossing - Length: 7.4 km - Non-stop time: 3 h - Altitude Differences: +280 - 140 m - Beauty: 3.

A short route connecting the village of Apéri with the beach of Aháta. The route follows an old partially preserved path that passes from the cave of Limniótis with the amazing geological decorations, continues to the little church of Agios Andréas and ends at the popular beach of Aháta.

Route 18
Spóa ❷⓿ - Mesochóri ❷❹

Type: Crossing - Length: 4.7 km - Non-stop time: 1 h 30' - Altitude Differences: +50 - 250 m - Beauty: 4

A really wonderful route, unknown to most hikers, that connects the villages of Spóa and Mesochóri. The weak point of this route is that two long sections near Spóa run on dirt road and asphalt. However, the part near Mesochóri is excellent. Some sections of the old pavement have survived.

NORTH KARPATHOS

The north part of the island (north of Spóa) is more sparsely populated and hiking is more attractive as there are lots of paths running in virgin areas and the relief of the ground is wilder but more fascinating.

North Kárpathos includes 12 hiking routes.

Route 1
Spóa ❷⓿ - Olympos ❷❶

Type: Crossing - Length: 16 km - Non-stop time: 5 h 30' - Altitude Differences: +570 - 660 m - Beauty: 2-first section & 4-second section.

This long route connects south with north Kárpathos. For hikers coming from the south, this is the entrance to the route network of Olympos. The first section is interrupted for 5 km by the roadway, which makes the route somehow boring and tiring. However, the hiker is rewarded in the second section, which runs towards Olympos along a well-made pavement above the steep west slopes of Profítis Ilías, and enters the famous village.

Route 2
Olympos ❷❶ - Péi ❷❷ - Olympos ❷❶

Type: Circular - Length: 13.1 km - Non-stop time: 4 h 45' - Altitude Differences: +370 - 340 m - Beauty: 3.

This circular route of the west coast visits Péi and returns to Olympos again via a long section of Route 1 (Spóa-Olympos). A very interesting route passing from the beach of Evgónymos and the little church of Agia Moní, where the hiker can also see Byzantine remains.

Route 3
Olympos ㉑ - Forókli Beach ㉓
(only descent)

Type: Return route - Length: 5.1 km - Non-stop time: 1 h 50' - Altitude Differences: +60 - 320 m - Beauty: 3.

The route starts from Olympos and runs down to the beach of Forókli. A beautiful route that runs alongside a stream with lots of water even in the summer. The isolated and undeveloped beach is bound to fascinate the hikers that can enjoy swimming undisturbed. A long and rough route that certainly discourages most hikers from using their car.

The problem is that the route is not connected with any other route and the hiker has to walk back uphill, which is very tiring especially in the summer.

Route 4
Diafáni ㉔ - Olympos ㉑

Type: Crossing - Length: 5.1 km - Non-stop time: 2 h 20' - Altitude Differences: +330 - 70 m - Beauty: 3.

The most common route connecting the port of Diafáni with Olympos. An interesting route that becomes even more charming when you walk uphill and start seeing Olympos below the imposing bulk of Profítis Ilías.

Route 5
Olympos ㉑ - Avlóna ㉕

Type: Crossing - Length: 4.8 km - Non-stop time: 1 h 45' - Altitude Differences: +190 - 150 m - Beauty: 3.

One of the most important routes of the network of north Kárpathos. The first section is very beautiful, especially when walked in the opposite direction, as the view of Olympos is incredible!

Route 6
Olympos ㉑ - Profítis Ilías Peak ㉖

Type: Crossing - Length: 2 km - Non-stop time: 1 h 35' - Altitude Differences: +459 m - Beauty: 4

A short but pretty route offering a panoramic view of the area from an altitude of 719 m and the little church of Profítis Ilías towering over the historic village. The route is mainly recommended for experienced hikers as it runs uphill along a very steep path.

Route 7
Olympos ㉑ - Agios Konstantínos Saddle ㉗ - Diafáni ㉔

Type: Crossing - Length: 6.8 km - Non-stop time: 2 h 30' - Altitude Differences: +70 m - 330 m - Beauty: 2 & 3.

This is the second route connecting Diafáni with Olympos but it is more interesting than the first one. Start from Olympos and reach the saddle of Agios Konstantínos before choosing one of the two routes that run down to Diafáni.

Route 8
Trístomo ㉘ - Avlóna ㉕

(in case you return, the following data doubles)

Type: Crossing - Length: 8.5 km - Non-stop time: 3 h 30' - Altitude Differences: +460 m - 180 m - Beauty: 3.

A charming route that leads to the north edge of the island. The lack of roads and the striking landscape make the hiker strongly feel that they move away from civilization and walk into a virgin area. For those walking from Avlóna, the view from the saddle above Trístomo is amazing.

The fact that at some points the old stone-made pavement has survived makes the route prettier. You have no other choice than to return via the same route unless a boat collects you from the coast.

Route 9
Avlóna ㉕ - Vroukoúnta Beach ㉙

Type: Crossing - Length: 4.1 km - Non-stop time: 1 h 25' - Altitude Differences: +10 m - 290 m - Beauty: 4.

This route gives the hiker the chance to visit ancient Vroukoúnta, one of the most beautiful places of the island. As it happens in Route 8, the lack of roads makes the visit more imposing, while the visitor is fascinated by the antiquities. Rock-cut tombs, Cyclopean walls and the little church of Ái-Giánnis under the rocks will really impress you!

Route 10
Avlóna ㉕ - Vanánta Beach ㉚ - Diafáni ㉔

Type: Triangular - Length: 5.8 km - Non-stop time: 2 h 10' - Altitude Differences: - 300 m - Beauty: 3.

The route connects the three above locations via a triangular path and offers the hiker the opportunity to walk from Diafáni to Avlóna and back. Long sections of the old paths have been destroyed by roads. A circular route is possible via two different paths.

Route 11
Diafáni ㉔ - Trístomo ㉘

Type: Crossing - Length: 10.6 km - Non-stop time: 4 h - Altitude Differences: +330 m - 330 m - Beauty: 4.

The most impressive and difficult route of the network as it runs along the steep east slopes to the north of Diafáni. Most sections of the old path have been damaged and it is very difficult for a hiker to discern it. See the stone-built staircase strangely called Ksylóskala (meaning wooden staircase) along the route. After the steep slopes, the route gets to a calmer place before it reaches the bay of Trístomo. Then the hiker may either continue straight to Trístomo or get at first to the little church of Agia Aikateríni behind the narrowest point of the canal separating Kárpathos from Saria and then to Trístomo. The second route is prettier, especially the view of the Strait from high above.

Route 12
Saría Island - Strait ㉛ - Old Settlement of Árgos ㉜ - Palátia ㉝

Type: Crossing - Length: 7.8 km - Non-stop time: 3 h - Altitude Differences: +240 m - 240 m - Beauty: 4.

The crossing of Saría starts from the south edge of the island and ends to the north. A route in a virgin environment that remains unforgettable to the hiker as the island has been preserved without dirt roads and interventions due to the settlement of Saracen pirates at Palátia but also due to the abandoned inland village of Árgos.

The round trip to Saría is by boat from Diafáni or Pigádia. Some boats visiting Saría leave the hikers to the south of the small island and sail to Palátia, where they collect them after the 3-hour hike.

Climbing

Climbing has also caught on in Kárpathos in recent years. Enterprises activating in alternative tourism and extreme sports have created suitable climbing fields with ready and positioned bolts and anchors on four coasts of the island. The level of difficulty follows the French climbing rating system:

• Kástello. The cape at the southernmost point of the island, behind the airport. 4 - 7a

• Ádeia. The beach of Pylés on the west side of the island. 4 - 6c

• Aháta. The pretty beach where the road from Apéri leads. 5 - 7b

• High (Vasilis paradise). Beach of north Kárpathos, access by sea. 5 - 8a

Information available at club mistral Karpathos, collaborator of ION CLUB, in Afiártis, Tel. No.: 2245091061, mail: karpathos@club-mistral.com, which gives lessons to aspirant climbers but also provides the necessary gear and transportation to the climbing fields.

Mountain Biking

The sport of mountain biking has spread in recent years in Greece and Kárpathos did not hesitate to participate in this activity. The club Anemos Scott MBT Center Karpathos proposes twelve routes (unsigned), between 25 and 60 km long, mainly along rural roads of different levels of difficulty depending on the technical training and endurance of the cyclists. It offers experienced cyclists as guides, technical support and, of course, the necessary equipment. Contact club Anemos Scott MBT Center Karpathos, collaborator of ION

CLUB, in Afiártis, Tel. No.: 2245091061, mail: karpathos@club-mistral.com

Wind surfing

Wind surfing is synonymous to Kárpathos for the lovers of the sport as between 2006 and 2009 the surf speed world championship was repeatedly held in the waters of Afiártis. The sea to the south of Kárpathos provides the ideal conditions for surfing with regard to both duration and intensity of winds. As a result, lots of businesses have been activating in Afiártis in recent years and are specialized in wind surfing while they also provide the surfers with infrastructures, equipment, know-how and, of course, lessons in this beautiful sport. The beaches of Afiártis, from the settlement of Kípos tou Afiárti as far as the airport, are full of the facilities of

Windsurfing facilities at Afiártis

the above businesses and the sea is crowded with colourful sails. Each beach and little cove is dedicated to a different level of difficulty.

• Makrýs Gialós or chicken bay: mainly for rookies and little children.

• Valiás or gun bay: the common and favourite field of surfers.

• Vathá or devil's bay or paradise bay: the sea field for speed surf lovers.

Businesses activating in wind surfing in the area of Afiártis are as follows:

• ANEMOS - ION Club: Makrýs Gialós, Afiártis, 2245091011

• Karpathos surf club: Makrýs Gialós, Afiártis, 6973474816.

• Pro Center Chris Schill: Vathá, Afiártis, 2245091062

The south beach of Agrilopótamos, situated 4 km to the west of the airport, accommodates BigDayz, which is specialized in kite surfing. The business provides anything a kite surfer needs in order to enjoy this exciting sport in the blue waters of the Libyan Sea, opposite the island of Kásos. BigDayz, Agrilopótamos, 22450110229

Diving

The seabed and the waters of Kárpathos are as rich and fascinating as its land. Besides, they have not been a random choice for the protected and rare Mediterranean monk seal monachus-monachus, which has selected Kárpathos as one of its favourite places for living and reproduction. There is very rich underwater life with wide biodiversity and extensive posidonia meadows. The relief of the seabed is also very impressive and includes reefs, colourful caves and deep gorges. There are also several wrecks, such as the reconnaissance aircraft Gernik of the German Luftwaffe, which was sunk in World War II sixteen metres under sea level at Diakóftis, behind the airport. Other wrecks include the cargo ship Días (Zeus), which has been lying twenty five metres under Diafáni since 1993, the yacht Spétses, sunk in 2007 near the beach of Agios Minás, and a Stuka German dive bomber, which was downed in 1943 near the beach of Agnóntia in north Kárpathos. In Pigádia you can find a diving centre, which will help you with underwater explorations with regard to transportation, gear and anything you might need, thanks to Dínos Protópappas, the Deputy Mayor from Olympos, who is responsible for the centre and an experienced diver himself with deep knowledge of his island.

Karpathos Diving Center, Pigádia (on the beach, below the provincial building), 2245022860, info@diving-karpathos.gr

Diving in the Karpathian Sea is spectacular

BEACHES

The lacy coastline of the island forms dozens of beaches, some with colourful pebbles and others with golden sand, all of them having crystal clear emerald waters. A great number of them are organized with deck-chairs and umbrellas as well as beach bars and taverns, while there are many more isolated and calm. In fact, the visitor can find over one hundred beaches in Kárpathos and Saría. Instead of tiring texts, we will present in a table the 60 most important of them together with all the necessary information you need in order to choose the one that caters your tastes. They are presented clockwise, starting from the north beach of the capital of Pigádia. Look up the maps of ROAD and ORAMA Editions that will greatly help you in searching and choosing the beach you like.

BEACHES

A journey in the Aegean sea

BEACHES

NAME	AREA	DISTANCE FROM PIGADIA	ORGANIZED	RESTAURANT / TAVERN	BEACH BAR	NATURAL SHADE	KIND	REMARKS
VRONTI	Pigadia	2	√	√			PEBBLE	
AFOTI	Pigadia	1	√	√	√		SAND	
PIGADIA	Pigadia	0	√	√	√		SAND	
AMMOS KSENONA	Pigadia	0	√	√	√		SAND	
POULIOU POTAMI	Ardani	7					PEBBLE	
MIKRI AMMOOPI	Ammoopi	8	√	√	√		SAND	
MEGALI AMMOOPI	Ammoopi	8	√	√			SAND	
VOTSALAKIA	Ammoopi	8	√	√			PEBBLE	
KASTELIA	Ammoopi	9	√				SLABS & PEBBLE	
FOKIA	Ammoopi	9				√	PEBBLE	
DAMATRIA	Afiartis	10	√	√	√		SAND	

Agios Theódoros

BEACHES

NAME	AREA	DISTANCE FROM PIGADIA	ORGANIZED	RESTAURANT / TAVERN	BEACH BAR	NATURAL SHADE	KIND	REMARKS
CHRISTOU PIGADI	Afiartis	11	√	√		√	SAND	
VATHA	Afiartis	14					FINE PEBBLE	wind surfing
VALIAS	Afiartis	15					SAND	wind surfing
MAKRYS GIALOS	Afiartis	16	√	√	√		SAND	wind surfing
DIAKOFTIS	Airport	18					SAND	climbing field
MICHALIOU KIPOS	Airport	19					SAND	
PSORIARI PLAKA	Airport	18					SAND	
POUNTA	Airport	19					SAND	
AGRILOPOTAMOS	South Karpathos	21	√	√	√		SAND	kite surfing
ARAKI	South Karpathos	23					FINE PEBBLE	
AGIOS THEODOROS	South Karpathos	25	√	√	√		PEBBLE	underwater fishing

BEACHES

Agios Minás

BEACHES

NAME	AREA	DISTANCE FROM PIGADIA	ORGANIZED	RESTAURANT / TAVERN	BEACH BAR	NATURAL SHADE	KIND	REMARKS
TRACHANAMMOS	Arkasa	23					PEBBLE	
TOICHIASMENAKI	Arkasa	24					SLABS	
AGIOS NIKOLAOS	Arkasa	16	√		√	√	SAND	beach volley
FOINIKI	Foiniki	18	√	√	√	√	SAND	
KAMARAKIA	Foiniki	19					SAND	
AGIOS GEORGIOS	Foiniki	20				√	PEBBLE	
PRONI	Pyles	22					PEBBLE	
ADEIA	Pyles	23	√	√			PEBBLE	climbing field
POTALI	Lefkos	33	√	√			PEBBLE	
GIALOU HORAFI	Lefkos	33	√	√	√	√	SAND	
PANAGIAS LIMANI	Lefkos	33	√		√		SAND	

BEACHES

Agrilopótamos

BEACHES

NAME	AREA	DISTANCE FROM PIGADIA	ORGANIZED	RESTAURANT / TAVERN	BEACH BAR	NATURAL SHADE	KIND	REMARKS
FRANGOLIMNIONAS	Lefkos	33	√	√			SAND	
PERDIKAS POTAMI	Lefkos	34					SAND	nudism
SAMAKI	Mesochori	31					PEBBLE	dirt road 2 km
MAKRYGIALOS	Mesochori	34					PEBBLE	dirt road 5 km
AGIA EIRINI	Mesochori - Spoa	X					PEBBLE	
VROUKOUNTA	Olympos	X					PEBBLE	hiking route
AGIOS SPYRIDON	Saria	X					PEBBLE	by sea
ALIMOUNTA	Saria	X					FINE PEBBLE	by sea
PALATIA	Saria	X				√	PEBBLE	by sea
MAEREIA	Saria	X					PEBBLE	by sea
VANANTA	Diafani	56				√	FINE PEBBLE	dirt road 2 km

KARPATHOS

BEACHES

Apella

BEACHES

NAME	AREA	DISTANCE FROM PIGADIA	ORGANIZED	RESTAURANT / TAVERN	BEACH BAR	NATURAL SHADE	KIND	REMARKS
DIAFANI	Diafani	53	√	√	√		PEBBLE	
PAPA MINA	East coast of north Karpathos	57					PEBBLE	dirt road 5 km
FOROKLI	East coast of north Karpathos	52				√	PEBBLE	dirt road 5 km
NATI	East coast of north Karpathos	41					PEBBLE	dirt road 4 km
AGIOS MINAS	East coast of north Karpathos	39	√	√			PEBBLE	dirt road 4 km
LALA	East coast of north Karpathos	X					PEBBLE	by seas
AGNONTIA	East coast of north Karpathos	42					PEBBLE	dirt road 5 km
HIGH	East coast of north Karpathos	X					PEBBLE	climbing field / by sea
AGIOS NIKOLAOS	Spoa	32	√	√	√		FINE PEBBLE	
AGIOS IOANNIS	Spoa	34					PEBBLE	dirt road 4 km
APELLA	East Karpathos	20	√	√		√	FINE PEBBLE	

BEACHES

Votsalákia

Agios Nikólaos

BEACHES

NAME	AREA	DISTANCE FROM PIGADIA	ORGANIZED	RESTAURANT / TAVERN	BEACH BAR	NATURAL SHADE	KIND	REMARKS
KYRA PANAGIA	East Karpathos	13	√	√			PEBBLE	
MAKRYS GIALOS KATODIOU	East Karpathos	13				√	PEBBLE	dirt road 1 km
KATO LAKKOS	East Karpathos	12				√	SAND	dirt road 1 km
AHATA	East Karpathos	11	√		√		FINE PEBBLE	climbing field

Aháta

KARPATHOS

BEACHES

Vrónti

The beach at Diafáni

BEACHES

Kyrá Panagiá

Potáli

BEACHES

Mikrí Ammoopí

Vanánta

A journey in the Aegean sea

BEACHES

Áfoti

The beach at Pigádia

BEACHES

Alimoúnta (Saría)

Palátia (Saría)

BEACHES

Christoú Pigádi

Náti

LOCAL CUISINE SHOPPING

The local dishes of Kárpathos are original and traditional, with strong influences from the tradition of the islands and neighbouring Crete. The most famous dishes are makaroúnes (local pasta) and vyzánti, which is goat or lamb meat, stuffed with rice and spices and cooked in the oven. Necessary supplement to the Karpathian meal is the psilokoúloura (rusks) with sesame as well as a great variety of breads, cakes and pastries rarely found in the Greek islands of the archipelago. You can find plenty of fish and seafood, mainly a certain type of squid, the so-called agriái, crabs, sea urchins and limpets, while the fish ménoula (blotched picarel), which looks like sardine, is dry salted. The gastronomic identity of the island is also described by the parrotfish, already known from antiquity, which is abundant only in the Karpathian Sea. You should taste it stewed or roasted with plenty of oil and lemon juice. The most famous

Making psilokoúloura *(photo: Maria Loízou)*

sweets are the Karpathian baklavá and sisamómelo (sesame seed candy). The Wine Festival in Lástos attracts lots of people who taste Adam's wine, as the locals call the wine they make in local wine presses on the celebration of Agios Geórgios Methystís, on November 3. On that day, they open the sealed barrels and the celebration is accompanied by wine and the charming sound of the lýra (lyre), the laoúto and the tsamboúna. Another alcoholic beverage is, of course, rakí (unsweetened, anise-flavored alcoholic drink). Here are the original recipes for two of the most typical dishes of Kárpathos as they were given to me by Ms Anna from Voláda, who is descended from Mesochóri.

.... **Makaroúnes** ....

Ingredients:
- black wheat flour
- yellow wheat flour
- Water
- salt
- onion
- olive oil
- butter
- grated cheese

Execution: *Mix the flour with the water and some salt so that the dough can rise and become thick. Knit thin threads of dough and pull them by hand, one at a time. Flour in warm water, add salt and boil while stirring. After a few minutes strain the water. Now you have to roast the onion, which has already finely been chopped. Roast it in olive oil, add some butter on the frying pan and, as soon as it has been roasted, add the makaroúnes. Sprinkle with cheese.*

.... **Vyzánti (or Fto)** ....

Ingredients:

- lamb or goat
- salt
- pepper
- Guinea pepper
- cumin
- ground cinnamon
- lemon
- onion
- butter
- rice
- water

Execution: *Wash the meat and rub it well with salt and lemon. In a frying pan roast the onion in butter and then add the finely chopped haslets of the animal. Put the rice in lukewarm water and add salt, pepper and the other spices. The water should not reach the boiling point. Stuff the belly of the animal with the mixture, stitch the opening with a needle and a special string, butter the exterior of the animal and add salt and pepper externally. Put it in a roasting pan and let it in the oven for 4-5 hours so that it can be roasted slowly.*

Shopping

Top quality thyme honey, caper, samphire, dry-salted ménoula (blotched picarel) from Spóa, red semi-sweet wine from Óthos, and do not forget psilokoúloura and local sweets like baklavá and sisamómelo (do not worry, they do not stale easily).

Apart from foodstuff, you can also buy stivánia (local boots) or even the entire traditional costume from Olympos as well as baskets and mastrapás (plural: mastrapádes meaning painted dishes) from Menetés. All of them are original and handmade products of local folk art.

ACCOMMODATION

There are more than 7,000 beds available on the island in approximately 200 tourist units. Most of them are based in Pigádia, especially along the beaches of the capital. A great number of rooms, apartments and hotels can be found inside the town as well. Apart from Pigádia, plenty of accommodation facilities also exist in Ammoopí and Lefkós. Olympos and Diafáni are two other villages where you can find accommodation, as it happens with the rest of the villages of the island, where you can stay in rooms, apartments or small hotels. They are very good value for money even in high season, while most of them offer breakfast and Wi-Fi connection. Below you can find a list of the places where you can stay and the necessary information for each of them at the time the present travel guide was published (Spring 2017).

NAME	STARS	AREA	TELEPHONE No.
AGIOS NIKOLAOS	2**	AGIOS NIKOLAOS	22450-71201
VOTSALO	2**	AGIOS NIKOLAOS	22450-71205
ALTHEA AMMOOPI	3***	AMMOOPI	
ALBATROS	3***	AMMOOPI	22450-81045
VOTSALAKIA	3***	AMMOOPI	22450-81198

ACCOMMODATION

NAME	STARS	AREA	TELEPHONE No.
HELIOS	3***	AMMOOPI	22450-81148
ARGO	2**	AMMOOPI	22450-81089
GALAZIA THALASSA	2**	AMMOOPI	22450-81036
KOLPOS AMMOOPIS	2**	AMMOOPI	22450-81184/5
OLYMPOS	2**	AMMOOPI	22450-81180
SOFIA	2**	AMMOOPI	22450-81078
VARDES	CLASS C	AMMOOPI	22450-81111
GALAZIA KYMATA	3***	APERIO	22450-23135
KYRA PANAGIA	3***	APERIO	22450-23026
B. & N. MELAS STUDIOS	2**	ARDANI	22450-81154
ARDANI BAY I	2**	ARDANI	22450-81026
ARDANI BAY II	2**	ARDANI	22450-81026
N. & B. MELAS STUDIOS	2**	ARDANI	22450-81154
ATHENA PALACE	4****	ARKASA	22450-61120
ARKASAS KOLPOS	4****	ARKASA	22450-61410
ARKESIA	3***	ARKASA	22450-61290
ARCHIPELAGOS	3***	ARKASA	22450-61342
DILINA	3***	ARKASA	22450-61103
THEA FINIKI	3***	ARKASA	22450-61400
POPI	3***	ARKASA	22450-61312
CHRYSOS HELIOS	3***	ARKASA	22450-61393
GIANNIS	2**	ARKASA	22450-61310
ELENI	2**	ARKASA	22450-61248

A journey in the Aegean sea

ACCOMMODATION

NAME	STARS	AREA	TELEPHONE No.
KALOKAIRINI AVRA	2**	ARKASA	22450-61483
AFIARTIS 2	3***	AFIARTIS	22450-23140
NEREIDES	4****	AFOTI	22450-23347
PARASOL	2**	AFOTI	22450-22923
ALPHA	2**	DIAFANI	22450-51280
GLAROS	2**	DIAFANI	22450-51501
BALASKAS	2**	DIAFANI	22450-51320
MAISTRALI STUDIOS	1*	DIAFANI	22450-51020
NIKOS	1*	DIAFANI	22450-51289
DIAKONIS	3***	ZETTES	22450-29081
AKTI LYMIATIS	3***	KARPATHOS	22450-22726
ASTRON	3***	KARPATHOS	22450-22774
VENETIA	3***	KARPATHOS	22450-22008
VERGINA	3***	KARPATHOS	22450-23501
KOLPOS POSSIRAMA	3***	KARPATHOS	22450-22916/8
MESOGEIOS	3***	KARPATHOS	22450-22213
MIRA MARE BAY	3***	KARPATHOS	22450-22345
SEVEN STARS	3***	KARPATHOS	22450-22101
OCEANIS	3***	KARPATHOS	22450-22975/6
AKTI ILIOU	2**	KARPATHOS	22450-22297
AMARYLLIS	2**	KARPATHOS	22450-22375
ANATOLI	2**	KARPATHOS	22450-22467
ATLANTIS	2**	KARPATHOS	22450-22200

ACCOMMODATION

NAME	STARS	AREA	TELEPHONE No.
GALAZIOS KOLPOS	2**	KARPATHOS	22450-22479
GALAZIOS ORIZON	2**	KARPATHOS	22450-22741
DELFINI	2**	KARPATHOS	22450-22665
EMBASSY	2**	KARPATHOS	22450-22671
THALASSINI PETRA	2**	KARPATHOS	22450-22897
IOLKOS	2**	KARPATHOS	22450-22192
LEFKA SPITIA	2**	KARPATHOS	22450-22973
MELTEMI	2**	KARPATHOS	22450-22829
MERTONAS	2**	KARPATHOS	22450-22622
BELVEDERE	2**	KARPATHOS	22450-22580
NISIOTIKOS HELIOS	2**	KARPATHOS	22450-22074
OASIS	2**	KARPATHOS	22450-22915
OLYMPIC	2**	KARPATHOS	22450-22708
PAVILION	2**	KARPATHOS	22450-22059
PANTHEON	2**	KARPATHOS	22450-22831
PANORAMA	2**	KARPATHOS	22450-22739
REGINA	2**	KARPATHOS	22450-22652
ROMANTICA	2**	KARPATHOS	22450-22460/1
TITANIA	2**	KARPATHOS	22450-22144
FOTEINI AKTH	2**	KARPATHOS	22450-22523
HARIS	2**	KARPATHOS	22410-22585
KARPATHOS	1*	KARPATHOS	22450-22347
YIALOS VILLAGE	3***	KATO LEFKOS	22450-71024

ACCOMMODATION

NAME	STARS	AREA	TELEPHONE No.
AEGEAN VILLAGE	4****	LAKKI KARPATHOU	22450-81194/5
ANEMOESSA	2**	LAKKI KARPATHOU	22450-81166
LAKKI BEACH	2**	LAKKI KARPATHOU	22450-81015
PERAMA	2**	LAKKI KARPATHOU	22450-81035
SKARPANTO	2**	LAKKI KARPATHOU	22450-81121
POTALI KOLPOS	3***	LEFKOS MESOCHORIOU	22450-71221
SARRIS INTERNATIONAL	3***	LEFKOS MESOCHORIOU	22450-71496
HORIO LEFKOS	3***	LEFKOS MESOCHORIOU	22450-71477
AURA STUDIOS	2**	LEFKOS MESOCHORIOU	22450-71115
ILIOVASILEMA	2**	LEFKOS MESOCHORIOU	22450-71171
THALASSINI MELODIA	2**	LEFKOS MESOCHORIOU	22450-71432
KRINOS	2**	LEFKOS MESOCHORIOU	22450-71410/2
MOUSSES	2**	LEFKOS MESOCHORIOU	22450-71484
NERAIDA	2**	LEFKOS MESOCHORIOU	22450-71461
SOCRATES	4****	LOTHIKO	22450-22590
XENIOS ZEUS	2**	LOTHIKO	22450-23493
PETRA STUDIO	2**	LOTHIKO	22450-22862
O FOINIKAS	1*	LOTHIKO	22450-29087
APOLIS	4****	MENETES	22450-81200
IRINI	3***	MENETES	22450-91000/1
CASTELIA BAY	2**	MENETES	22450-22678
POSEIDON	2**	MENETES	22450-91066
MIRALUNA	3***	MESOCHORI	6973575371

KARPATHOS

ACCOMMODATION

NAME	STARS	AREA	TELEPHONE No.
ALIMOUNDA MARE	5*****	PIGADIA	22450-23007
KONSTANTINOS PALACE	5*****	PIGADIA	22450-23401
ALMYRA HORIO	4****	PIGADIA	22450-29075
ASTRON PRIGKIPISSA	4****	PIGADIA	22450-29205
ICHOS TIS THALASSAS	4****	PIGADIA	22450-29023
AKTI ELECTRA	3***	PIGADIA	22450-22577
AIOLOS (EOLOS STUDIOS)	2**	PIGADIA	22450-23138
ALEX	2**	PIGADIA	22450-22004
EPIPHANY	2**	PIGADIA	22450-22136
THEA AIGAIOU	2**	PIGADIA	22450-29020/2
ILIAS (ELIAS ROOMS)	2**	PIGADIA	22450-22788
NISIA	2**	PIGADIA	22450-29127/8
PLAZA	2**	PIGADIA	22450-22713
FILOXENIA	2**	PIGADIA	22450-22182
CHORIO TIS KARPATHOU	2**	PIGADIA	22450-23296
ZOE	CLASS C	PIGADIA	22450-22033
APOLLO	2**	PYLES	22450-23351
ODYSSEY	2**	SISAMOS	22450-23240/2
ALKIONI	3***	FOINIKI ARKASAS	22450-61266
ARHONTIKO	2**	FOINIKI ARKASAS	22450-61473

** The information about the hotels is provided by the Hellenic Chamber of Hotels for the year 2017.

A journey in the Aegean sea

USEFUL NUMBERS

NAME	AREA	TELEPHONE No.
TOWN HALL	PIGADIA	2245022427
PROVINCIAL BUILDING	PIGADIA	2245022116
KARPATHION DROMENA / KOPAP	PIGADIA	2245060146
POLICE	PIGADIA	2245022222
POLICE	DIAFANI	2245051213
PORT AUTHORITIES	PIGADIA	2245022227
PORT	DIAFANI	2245051227
CUSTOMS	PIGADIA	2245022225
CUSTOMS	DIAFANI	2245051290
HEALTH CENTRE	PIGADIA	2245022228
MEDICAL STATION	OLYMPOS	2245051201
MEDICAL STATION	ARKASA	2245061204
CATHEDRAL	APERI	2245031222
FIRE BRIGADE	APERI	2245023676
AIRPORT	AFIARTIS	2245022305
TRAVEL AGENCY	PIGADIA	2245022235
TRAVEL AGENCY	PIGADIA	2245022778
TRAVEL AGENCY	DIAFANI	2245051316
POST	PIGADIA	2245022119
ACS COURIER	PIGADIA	2245023332
SPEEDEX COURIER	PIGADIA	2245022069
GENIKI TACHYDROMIKI COURIER	PIGADIA	2245023900
ALPHA BANK	PIGADIA	2245022330
NATIONAL BANK	PIGADIA	2245027003
PIRAEUS BANK	PIGADIA	2245022003
HOTELS ASSOCIATION	PIGADIA	2245022483
ELIN PETROL STATION	ARKASA	2245300501
EKO PETROL STATION	VRONTIS	2245023114
EKO PETROL STATION	VRONTIS	2245022910
EKO PETROL STATION	PIGADIA	2245022489
RADIO TAXI	PIGADIA	2245022705
PUBLIC BUS	PIGADIA	2245022338
SFAKIANAKIS TRANSPORT	PIGADIA	2245023229
GEORGOUSAKIS TRANSPORT	PIGADIA	2245022850

AFTERWORD

I would like to dedicate the afterword to a great number of Karpathians whom I did not mention as it would seem to be irrelevant to a travel guide. The expatriate Karpathians! They are exactly double their brothers who live on the island but they love it equally, if not more than them. These people are part of Kárpathos' soul and I could not fail to mention them. Emigration from the island started towards the late 19th c. and the people mainly left for Greece (Kárpathos was under Turkish occupation at the time) and the Middle East. In the early 20th c. until 1924 a great number of people migrated to the USA, while the same happened between 1964 and 1970. However, apart from America, the Karpathians also migrated to Australia, Canada, even Zimbabwe in Africa! A large community lives in Attica of Greece, mainly in Piraeus. The overwhelming majority are settled in America, over ten thousand Karpathians, as compared to the seven thousand living on the island. Baltimore comprises a second Olympos! Large communities also exist in New Jersey, Montreal of Canada as well as in other areas of America. Like all other Greeks living abroad, the Karpathians prospered in their new countries and became prominent in all sectors of social life. They became very supportive of their island by founding dozens of clubs through which they have tried to maintain their cultural

identity, honour their origin and hand these values down to the next generations of Karpathians. They also help their country on every occasion by donating and mainly investing on the island, while they regularly visit their beloved Kárpathos for as much as they can, even in their summer holidays. A surge of return to the fatherland had been noticed until some years ago, but unfortunately it stopped because of the continuing economic crisis in Greece. However, because they make colossal offers to the island, the Municipality of Kárpathos has given their name to the main footwalk of Pigádia, above the beach, which is now called Street of Expatriate Karpathians.

(photo: Maria Loízou)

BIBLIOGRAPHY REFERENCES

- KARPATHOS & KASOS, A FOLKLORE PARADISE
  (G. DESYPRIS - TOUMBIS, 2001)
- KARPATHOS (COLLECTIVE - ADAM)
- 50 BEACHES OF KARPATHOS (COLLECTIVE - HELIANTHOS, 2013)
- KARPATHOS, MAGNIFICENT BLUE (CHRIS. STEFANAKIS)
- DISCOURSE ON THE GEOLOGY OF KARPATHOS (G.PANTOPOULOS, 2006)
- OLYMPOS, KARPATHOS
  (COLLECTIVE - CENTRE FOR KARPATHIAN STUDIES, 2015)
- VISITOR'S GUIDE (MANAGING BODY OF KARPATHOS - SARIA)
- KARPATHOS: OPERATIONAL PLAN ON DEVELOPMENT 2014 - 2020, (SOUTH AEGEAN REGION 2014)
- www.menetes.org
- www.syllogoskarpathion.com
- www.kynoclub.gr
- www.karpathiaki.gr